I like Moore's poems because, like that particular sacred romance, they have happy cosmic endings.

— *Abdallah Schleifer*

Daniel Moore's poetry is the exercise of the divine, an open gate to the wilderness of the eternal. Every word possesses a sacred space, every image confirms the reality of the invisible.

— *Munir Akash*

Daniel Moore, even though he's been writing for so many years, has yet to be discovered. He's writing from such a wide and diverse platform that it may take a truly new and truly global "fifth world" citizen to hear where he's coming from.

— *Hakim Archuletta*

### Praise for The Ramadan Sonnets

Poets' pens soar when they are free but disappear when they are effective. Daniel Moore's poems soar long after the ink has dried and the pen lifted. From feasts in Fes to desserts in the desert, Daniel takes us on a trip of which the best guide happens to be a consummate poet. He is that guide.

— *Hamza Yusuf Hanson*

The litany of the beautiful Ramadan Sonnets may seem to be opposed to that of Khayyam's Rubaiyat, yet its aim may be the same: *Liberation.*

— *Lawrence Ferlinghetti*

# THE BLIND BEEKEEPER

# THE BLIND BEEKEEPER

POEMS

•

## DANIEL MOORE

*For Shulamith
a lovely round robin
flew today!
Daniel Moore
5/17/03*

*A JUSOOR BOOK*

A Jusoor Book
Published by
**Kitab**
Bethesda, Maryland


Cover design: Munir Akash

ISBN:0-9652031-4-X

First edition
2001

Many thanks to the editors of the publications
in which the following poems appeared:
*Solo*: The Face of Death; *Jusoor*: The Blind
Beekeeper, The Day the Earth Stood still;
*Nexus*: Allen Ginsberg Dead at 70.


This book is available to bookstores through
**Syracuse University Press**
621 Skytop Road, Suite 110
Syracuse, NY 13244-5290 USA
Tel (for orders only): (800) 365-8929
Fax: (315) 433-5545,
email: talitz@syr.edu / twalsh01@syr.edu

Printed in the United States of America

# CONTENTS

In a single life so many soulful cosmoses appear, each an echo from their Creator, so I want to thank Munir Akash among them for his unflagging support, Kamala Cesar for her kind generosity in helping to publish this book, and dedicate these buzzing poems to my wife Malika and our children Farid and Salihah.

# THE BLIND BEEKEEPER

بِسْمِ اللَّهِ الرَّحْمَنِ الرَّحِيمِ

Your Lord reveals to the bees:
   "Build dwellings in the mountains and the trees,
      and also in the structures which men erect.
   Then eat from every kind of fruit
      and travel the paths of your Lord,
   which have been made easy for you to follow."
From inside them comes a drink of varying colors,
   containing healing for mankind.
There is certainly a sign in that for people who reflect.
                     — *Qur'an, Sura 16:68- 69*

He to whom time is the same as eternity,
and eternity the same as time, is free of all
adversity.
                     — *Jacob Boehme*

# CABBAGE

The sky is black and the moon is a
cut fingernail scallop tossed up

illuminated perfect clarity people
passing underneath all emblematic glow

into houses, hovels, hearts on fire.
There's an enormous movement within

all of us. It has a rumble sound,
hydraulic tilt, it has a weightlessness

deep as history, more full of
colorful characters, charades, candle-lit

observances, star-light in constellatic
patterns, animals in the distance

roaring at feeding time, waking up
every neighbor within miles.

It's what pounds on the door impatiently,
it's what sits in a saintly light

under windows of tropic rainbows.
It gnashes beautiful teeth.

It's bigger and smaller than
we are. We

come out in the moonlight to meet it.
Hello heart light. Tiger face.

11/15/96

1

## GREEN LIGHT

Green light falls among tendrils.

Coils of yellow rootlets twist around sticks.

Leaves push out from centers. Flowers.

Foxes huddle in dens. Dark.

Sunlight falls in brown strips.

Deep night covers half the planet. Dense.

The desert's indistinguishable in the night.

You wouldn't know it went for miles.

A camel skull sits in the sand. Eye sockets.

Moon light.

11/20

2

## WINTER HAIKU

Winter's on its way.

Maple leaves all

cross the street together.

11/22

## SEVEN THUNDERS

Seven Thunders ring their bells

(I'm using the Blakean mode).

Gates of Joy clank open on smooth rollers.

Fiery clouds hang over the Skuylkill River.

Outlines of light shimmer in black sky.

11/29

## GLEAMS

Fragrant fragments. Velveteen.
Voice like a rainbow. Gleams
in the night. Traffic swerving.
The sure hand on the handle.

Stanza two. Hand like a claw
gripping the pen. Up in the head
the cups on the wall
fall. Let in little light.

All right. We're at the corner
of Picadilly. What
does it matter. I'll
go, she said, and toddled
off. The door blew
open. The wind stood.

Hat in hand. Loose sand. Storm.
Curtain obscuring. Thin
film over everything.
Velveteen. Soup tureen.
Gleams.

11/30

# LOTS OF SAD HARMONICAS

Lots of sad harmonicas
are playing out back.

Seems the widow Jenkins
won't come out to play.

Seems the basic killer in all of us
has gone too far.

Seems this town ain't what it
used to be, and it

never was.

12/7

## HOE-DOWN

Lockjaw of the Heart stood up to the microphone
but when he finally opened his mouth
dead birds fell out of the rafters,
cobwebs unmade themselves thread by thread
and the glue on the chairs bled down to the
ground, deconstructing the carpentry.

Evil Actions Guilty Thoughts got up to save the
day but he was so angular to the visible, so
deflected by his own being, that
even though hollering like a pig-caller
no one could hear him. He couldn't even
hear himself.

Then Deep Dumb Darkness approached the mike.
He knew he could belt out a song that would
win peoples' hearts. Oh boy!
But as soon as his larynx began twanging,
the sound of buzz saws and gigantic machinery
clanking and wheezing
burst everyone's eardrums.

12/11

7

# NIGHTMARE

The memory I've retained of it
starts when I am told to take the
head home in a brown paper bag
it's a green cabbage
but it somehow is also a severed head
and it has the will and spirit of a
live head still in it
so I recall trying to get the
cabbage into the large brown shopping bag
trying to force it into the dark opening
and it somehow refusing
I tried to force it this way and that but like
the wrong end of a magnet it would
be propelled away from the opening
the atmosphere began to get scary
I talked to the head
I actually was standing over the head
commanding it to get in the bag
I started speaking rather firmly
I shouted at the cabbage
and finally it complied
I picked up the bag with the
    cabbage inside
and was about to carry it
into a dark and clammy street so late and
    lonely at night
the bag with the alive head in it in my
    hands
and as I started out
suddenly the sniffing, huffing, audible
nasty breathing of demons and
    bad spirits closed in on me
surrounded me and made my
    flesh crawl
I've got goosebumps again now

just writing it
and the fright was so intense at this
    point that I
woke up
scared out of my wits
having to turn on the light
pray for protection
pray God for protection against
  the evil of Satan
with all my heart
before I could go back to sleep.

12/11

## MOROSE

OK, the patient's ailing —
a black eagle's unfolded hard wings above his head —

his body's got oceanic breakers all around it,
he's sinking into rock, his heart is dead.

Snakes from the other world are slithering along his ankles.
His eyesockets are cinerama theaters of hallucination.

A cruel ripple's working its way upward.
At the center of his being's an unknown destination.

## ON THE LABEL

This life wasn't made:
"*meant to last.*"

## STATEMENT OF WITNESS

*"There is no God ..."*

Pause. Silence. Years go by and some
   intrepid souls actually
write books about it, fill a so-called
vacuum with their squeals of despair,
scratch their heads incessantly, scratch
   each other's heads.

But then the voice takes another
   breath, for breath is the
current the canoes of words go out on, and
finishes the sentence:

*"but God."*

12/14

## RECOGNITION

The same God Who sent the prophets
and inspired the Qur'an

has me work at a job I hate
then come home and wash the dishes.

12/14

## RENEWAL

I would have perfect pink mermaids
   balancing on their tails on
translucent blue conch shells
for my renewal.

Men, and women too,
love to gaze on beautiful mortal
forms, to
   remind them of eternity.
*"The Human
Form Divine,"* Blake said. Their

mermaid faces fluctuating
   somewhere between huge-eyed
faces of gazelles and transparent
   faces of angels, like clouds seen
down below from windows of airplanes, luminous
   miles of dazzling immateriality like
puffy mattresses you feel you could
   bail out on and bounce, rather than
hurtle through to a pain-wracked, though
   probably painlessly unconscious
      death.

*"For my renewal,"* I said, after anguish.
A pulse pushes the sides of the wound together like
pursing lips to praise God in every state,
to sing in an empty seaside resort so the
   song resounds among solitary
      shower stalls. Echoes. Calling to the

mermaids gradually coming into view, in symmetrical
choreography more perfect than a 50's
   Esther Williams movie, all their
lips also shell-like in praise's oval shapes,

song wafting out across strewn debris,
a few skeletons sticking out of the sand,
white xylophone keys reflecting dark moonlight.

And then creatures join in when renewal
pushes out its tides, antelope and deer,
several species of bird, fanning tails so
bright just God can look on them and
    not go blind.

And we go blind with love and laughter
after the tornado's torn the town to bits,
raising fists in defiance or our
glasses to toast the Power that
    beat us, to feel those

giant ribs squeezing our sides, to know there's
something so much greater than we are
that while we're unable to conceive of it
is telling us its name.

That while we're rolled out by its rolling pin
we're happily receiving its messages,
for all that we are or have.

12/16

# CORRESPONDENCES

The curve of an "s" and the curvature of a spine,

a turtle's head and an old politician's,

a road going up and a hand making gliding motions,

a redhead in a convertible and a red-tipped
   moth's wing in a rain forest,

the headless horseman and a guy head-over-
   heels in love with something
      more than his own self image,

a dust mote and a dust mite,

a court dwarf and a sudden thought,

a balmy day and the ocean's sigh,

the length of this poem and a
   worm extending itself — how long?

a flight of canaries and an old wife
   chattering to herself,

a car full of immigrants and the language
   full of metaphors,

the seashore and a teenager's bedroom,

this list extending infinitely and an
old professor racking his brains to bring
   Homer to life to another
class of odoriferous undergraduates,

a moving train in Kansas and a vulture's
   shadow running along
      curvaceous Sahara dunes,

the most populous city in the world and the
   Oxford Unabridged Dictionary,

newspapers open in the early morning London
subway and white butterflies opening and
   closing their wings in the sun,

children in a toy store and old Zen
   Buddhists pouring tea,

color crayons and wild flowers on a
   Mediterranean hillside,

the love of God and planet earth seen from a distance
   in endless space,

the stars in the sky and great ideas in a
      single person's lifetime,

coming back to where we came from and
   hikers surviving Himalayan peaks,
      hoping for hot coffee,

this poem finding its way in the dark and a
forest antelope cautious about tigers,

I don't want to stop and I can't go on,
and the angel needing to tend to somebody else
      somewhere.

12/27

# THE FACE OF DEATH

I've looked upon the face of death
of my white haired wife asleep
and it was flocks of white geese landing
   feet first on lakes of a deep deep blue
so dark as to be darker than the
      covering night, with
ten times as many stars in its depths,
and my wife's face a profile more lunar than that
lifeless orb in earth's thrall, her

spirit against the lids of her material flesh
more alive than the leap of new gazelles at
   first light,
her heart across the mileage of that lake
more adept at balance than any
man-made craft, and death is itself
a message from beyond, it
shows us the work on its shield, the
   etching in deep grooves on its glass,
for a moment in sleep, her eyes sunken in, her
      mouth agape, my heart

reached a low chord on the scale to think of her
gone. In a lament's

burnished corner, brown wood and the
red glow of a hearth, confronted by grief.
Knowing her release.

Death is a white boat on a black lake,
a white moon on a black highway,
a white dish on a black table,
a white paper with black script writing
   this poem with my
own death flowing out the tip of this pen

as my wife lies asleep by my side
in the quiet room.

                              12/29

# HARP DREAM

In the dream I secured a perfect little
  harp, it was translucent
    white, made of that
high class plastic on backs of expensive
  hair brushes from the 1920's,
tiny metal strings, but all in tune,

I grabbed it off the pile of things leaned all
    together in the antique junkyard I'd been
exploring with lots of other people, rummaging through
interesting objects,

the dream began by my coming onto a hilltop fenced-in
junkyard and spying over the
fence a bunch of Victorian picture frames,
dark carved wood with ornate
flowers and gewgaws, I asked someone on the
inside to do me a favor, hand me over those
frames, which he said he'd do if I
  paid him, and I agreed, he
handed over three frames, I asked if there were
any more, he asked what
size I wanted, I gestured, said
  large was OK, then I was

inside the junkyard myself, and found some
wonderful things I can't recall, I had a
  stash somewhere I would go
    back to with my treasures, then I
discovered a pile of old harps, smaller than
Irish harps, and found one that was
  broken, with some strings still attached, but
no base, I left it and went on to
  other things, then suddenly felt I
wanted it and went back, I

20

turned a corner and there was this perfect
white plastic Art-Deco fully strung
　　harp where there
　　　hadn't been one before, I
took it and maybe the broken one too,

(I recall thinking about paying the first guy I saw
five dollars, hoping it was enough, but thought, well,
　　junkyard people are cheap),

people were rushing out of the yard now,
I saw lots of people scrambling
　　over the fence as if the police
were coming, I looked out across the
open field and saw nothing, but
there was such a knowing
exodus of people in brightly colored
　　junkyard clothes that I also
picked up my harps and ran as fast as I
　　　could, clambering over the
fence and out of the yard. Then I was on a

bridge across some water, strumming my
perfect harp, and the
　　dream ended.

1/1/97

## SINGLE HEARTBEAT

Sea-sparkle, a dazzling sequined hat,
　rock-jut, prehistoric beasts underneath
　　cutting up through dirt,

sky-stretch across the space of a glance, one
　glance enough to
　　encompass the all, the whole

elk and all its antlers, the whole
earth and all its people encircling a
　still center, round and round
　　a still center,

night blackness, the tired mind shutting down,
the body, independent principalities with
　separate governments, in one skin,

the act of breathing, in a little compass, only the
　air of circular lamplight
available for immediate usage,

miles and miles of knowledgeable men and
　women in coarse robes with
　　long books full of live words

　　like flaming butterflies leaving
dry brown pages to fill the sky of the
　mind's heart in a

　　single heartbeat.

## IF SPACE IS ACTUALLY

If space is actually a convergence of
    giant holes
with an angel of blue light suspended
    in each one trembling with
        energy, electrical
    twinkle at any moment able to
elongate into terrible lightning, but high-pitched
    song instead that
        vibrates the distant
leaves of trees being the vehicle of
choice for these stunning creatures —

If rather than being in one place at one time,
place and time themselves are a
    series of intercommunicating and
        interconnecting dream-visions with
unknown starting points and no known
    ending, so that
horses transforming into treetops into
    housing developments into the
        smile on a little girl playing
            jacks in a sun-shaft
are as natural as
the lilt of an aria going into crunch-sounds, into
    waterfall-swoosh, earthshaking
catastrophe with attendant rumbles and
    screams turning suddenly into the
tiny ripple effect on the surface of
coffee in a cup when a train goes by, shaking the
    entire tenement building,

and the space angel stretched to the circumference of the
space-hole is apparent in a
large but sweet explosion in the
heart at the gong-sound of truth

told by an infant into the ear of a Mongolian grandfather
whose beard is draped over the
snowy heights of Himalayan peaks

in a pure blue sky
in a day with no wind

in a
night without end...

1/5

# IN THE LONG RUN

The owl is only as wise as the
  person who looks on it with
    wisdom-thoughts (though I say
an owl among owls is only as
  wise at it need be).

The blue sky above the minaret
has a blue on the skirt of the Turkish princess
that's only as blue as the heron's
  underwing when extended over
    Aleppo.

The river Po rushes only as fast as the
river Po needs to flow in order to
go where the river Po needs to go.

It's black as night, with the sun coming up
only as fast as the members of the
  attacking army saying their mental
    prayers, licking their lips and
going over procedures in their minds, shifting
the weight of heavy equipment from
one shoulder to the other, saying goodbye
in their minds to their loved ones
as the sky lightens, taking deep breaths
softly to themselves and
closing their eyes.

The mouse in the wall
is only as timorous as a blade of wheat
in early morning breeze, flittering
  this way and that, trembling its
golden stalk in the dawn's fresh air.

The unseen creatures all around us, above and

below us, are unseen only by us,
seers of material things, missing
the evil-seeing fiery eye of the demon, the
soft smiled sweet-seeing angel bringing down rain,
the wild-eyed djinn's smoky hair and sliding movements
as it streaks through time, riding
time like a wing'd stallion.

I am only as full of despair and frustration,
only as full of fear of the Judgement's
   outcome, as God
      wants me to be, churning and
churning in my heart the same
   grievances and obsessions
            over and over, praying for
         relief.

Our lives are only as long as our
   lives have been decreed to be,

sitting 5:30 AM on the edge of my
bed with its black sheets in my
new green flannel pajamas writing in a
longhand that may not be all that

      long in the long run.

1/5

26

# PEWTER GLEAM

The pewter gleam that Jacob Boehme saw,
the *Glad Day* beaming joy of William Blake,
Thomas Traherne's childlike
   light-beams of Paradise,

the light in this room, diffuse yet singing,
the strong light of the sensitive voice of thought that
  arcs from California to Philadelphia by
    telephone from soul-brother
  recently back from the
      living and dead saints of Mauritania,

who don't stand in the way of the light —
the more they have died to their
  selves and have
   let their selves die
the more they are alive —

and I sit with them on a green hillside at dusk
drinking tea out of small gold-rimmed glasses,
and the sunlight gleams on the tea-light and
  spreads tea-light on the
ground from God's unending generosity to His
     creatures.

1/9

27

## WHAT IS IT OUTSIDE OF US

What is it outside of us that will
   sing the song of our souls?
What songbird so catch the
   upward ray of our longing in its
glorious throat and carry it to where
   gold light tints the outsides of clouds?

What movie so catch our fancy in its
   net that we see
      ourselves looking back at us from the
screen, from all those silvery flecks
   that reflect back the projected
image as it flitters across then darts back into
      blackness? What

rock star or pop star so speak our
language that our own language find
   refuge in its
      reproducible excitement?

What blond angel come before us with a
baby's glowing face, carrying torches of green and yellow
supernatural light, speaking words that so
poignantly draw us upward out of our own
   craws, throat-fishing down in the
      heart-well, pulling up
   deep heart's desire, giving it
      wings or melody or litany of
   words rich enough to
propel it out of all imagining?

And then, is it actually only outside us that
this kind of inspiration comes, these
   glass bells strung
      out along the

vacant feelings of our need for
a true representative of our
      innermost ambiguities
made suddenly clear?

The more radiant the prophet be outside us
the more deep within we find
      resonant unity.

A voice like a flute of
   raw amber come
      striding slowly out of a
   thick forest with trees so alive they seem
unbelievable.

At this moment now,
   facing us,

you are alive.

1/10

## LITTLE POCKETS OF AMBITION

Gypsy smoke, minds that won't
    develop past a certain point, dwell
      in a blue box, alienate grasshoppers,
the shadow of steamboats on
    greasy water, the
  narrative faculty
      wasted when put to
        too prosaic use, needing
      a golden palm tree or two to
        bloom and prosper in
          all that aridity,

the volume of unsent love letters to those
    unspent lips of yours, they
      actually lounge in their
        chairs, actually lie
      back topless with a wet glisten,
        invitational, arousing
      both my lust and my suspicions,
(leftist leanings among university students in
    Warsaw, rightist
      leanings among doctors already in
        surgery, having their
tongues removed, replacing an
    eyeball),

or, as at the beginning of this
tirade to my shadow against a
wall of insecurity,

gypsy smoke, blue twists against a
    black sky that seems to go
on forever, unto
far planetoids, far asteroids,

where no shadow but the one fastened
tight to the far
  shadow-side
    dwells to
disturb our tranquility.

1/5

## GREEK ISLES

Leafy white islands afloat in a blue sea
in the round eyes of a sculpted stone face
come alive in a ray of green sunlight
sitting atop a silver table on a
  multi-columned esplanade

overlooking the blue sea of the first line
whose braiding breezes are of musk and
  tamarind combined, marjoram and garlic
blown sweet by white sea breezes come from
as far as the Sahara, overland, through

sky so blue sapphires gaze into it to
adjust their color.

While underneath this fictitious description of a
real place I've never been to, but a
place embedded through travel posters and
  glossy cigarette ads in my
memory washed up on the shores of
  Western Civilization somehow
coming to us in Greek togas and a
democracy that actually only worked in
  Greece for a few years, maybe
not even a century, struts the panoply of
  tyrants, Caesars,
    enslavement, megalomania,
    oppression of women, the
usual diet of human foibles, erected to
    positions of fabulous power,

while turquoise sea-water laps
  prows of pointed white ships,

and grizzled old Greeks with raucous roving

eyes and a day's growth
mend their sails for tomorrow

in the cool evening's lengthy
    bronze sunset.

1/18

## INFINITE SADNESS

I want to express infinite sadness.

How should I go about it?

Should I dip a whole life's tragedy
  like a big spoon through the
    roof of their house and pull up
the last of the survivors? The lone
child with big eyes, the good-hearted
    grandmother?

Should I wait until after midnight and
  stand on a seashore somewhere
face to the black night sucking up
    volumes of black sea? Or just

stand on a street corner as the waters of the
ocean of human life go down to the
sea bottom where wrecks of
homeless people on steam grates lie?

The thief who takes a few pieces of
    disposable junk rather than
  the rajah's pearl, a

killer who takes the whole beating heart of a
    life for no good reason and
so throws his own life down a brink that
yawns so wide it actually
encompasses part of our lives as well.

Lace from a ripped bodice, splattered with
  blood.

Hair in bunches, torn out.

34

Empty buildings, their windows
   blown out.

Lives, still walking, their spirits like
  old candles
     blown out.

I want to play a low harp note
that will be heard far and wide.
The waters of the heart
   felt in the sidelong angles of the
      chest, corners
where tears don't reach, where words
   hardly come.

That touches us all.

An ache in the body
   that doesn't leave us.

Heartache.

1/23

## DO NOT CURSE TIME

If time were a piece of licorice you could
suck on until it ran out,

or a pair of loose suede shoes you could
walk in until they fell apart,

or a trail up an inclined plane you could
  take until you got
    where you wanted to go,

a small white horse you could
ride sometimes or have walk beside you,

if time were a constant rubbing sound,
    softer than sandpaper, that gave you a
      kind of shuffling rhythm
  wherever you went,

if time were a big black coat like
highwaymen used to wear which would
billow out all around you very
dramatically, like a
    great tent with legs,

if time were a place you could sit
    until you wanted to move on,

a comb you could run through your
    hair until the
comb broke or your hair fell out,

if time were a place that sold a
    certain kind of food, very
      hot and spicy, leaving a
long sweet aftertaste,

if time were a pack animal like a
    llama from the Andes, with
great wet eyes, gentle disposition and
        warm wool,

if time were a particularly poignant
conversation with a friend who would
    soon be leaving forever,

a native boat with great balsa pontoons
that catches each bronze sunset on the
white screen of its sail,

a song that goes as long as the
    singer can hold out,

if time were all these things (waiting
    for a fish to bite or an elk to
        appear at the crest of a hill),
or only one of them,

but time is this
uncanny component of
the space we are in, it is too loose and
    invisible, its durations are too
        elusive and subjective, some things take
forever to go by, some things are
    gone as soon as you
        grasp them, it's
too large, too boundaryless, we're
in it like snowmen slowly melting,

we're in it like a movie that
    should be playing in
        front of us, but it's
all around us and we're the
central character, clicking by at

enough rate to
    animate the proceedings,

so it's time that keeps the active ones active,
cuts down the ones whose time it is
    to be cut down,

that watches the fern uncurl its green
fist and turn into a green plume,

that takes us further and further away from
    such things as The Flood, the
      invention of the light bulb,
the moment of our conception, the
    day of our birth, we
sail away from them and hardly have
    time to wave goodbye when we're
      out on the open sea
with dolphins darting in and out of our wake
    under an implacable white sun,

it's time that makes the pastry delicious
    then turns it green with mold,

it's time that gives the lanky child wisdom
    as it looks up with careful eyes
and gazes into our soul with the
    hint of a smile,

a lone bird sails on its currents,

radio-waves leapfrog in great rings
over its spaces,

tiny praying mantises burst out of a pod and
    populate the garden with
      devotional

insects who eat dangerous and pesky
    insect invaders
  as well as their own devotional lovers,

it's time in all this
aligned as it is with space, or rather

not aligned, that suggests a
  parallel reality, when actually
without time space would be a black
    dot going nowhere,

without time space would be one thought and one
  thought only, and we'd
    never know what it is,

whereas now we actually do know the
  thought space is thinking
    moment by moment
and what is
momentarily going through its heart

as we look all around us
sucking on a licorice

watching the last golden flicks of nearby angel wings
disappear above the horizon.

1/25

## CONSCIOUSNESS AFTER DEATH

If consciousness continues after death
then I shall take this moment with me
   when I go.
I'll take the whole balloon of spirit I'm
   now in, and all its content,
details, masked and unmasked events
   in which I danced with cobras
      on a sea of glass,
or dreamed I danced. I'll take my

sleeplessness and moment of awaking, my
love of the awakened ones for whom
no mountain peak is too high to be
   excluded from their intimate vision,
a constant screen of falling lights behind
   them as they walk, or
      sit and talk.

I'll take my loves with all their
   blue smoke and golden moments,
my mental lusts as well I guess, zebras munching
   tall grass, stopping
     to blink at us, then
     returning to their munching.

Sensual obsessions
dragged kicking and screaming into the arena,
stripped naked and shown to be only
   blond bamboo bending in
     too many breezes. Our desires also like
beautiful black orchids
   battered by the very winds that
     so enhanced them at the first.
Burned by the very lights they set on fire.

Leaving only a fine ash in the
    shape of orchids, fine ash in the
        shape of bamboo. A spirit moving
freed among them, liberated from
    pretense and subterfuge, sweet as a
lone mouse discovered between walls. This

free spirit I'll take with me when I go
if consciousness continues after death.

This freedom from attachments,
moving as a space unencumbered into
pure unencumbered space!

Space into space,
    consciousness into
        consciousness,

the defined and definite into
    even greater definition,
next world of shadowless clarity

(water glass suspended in air
defined by the air it's suspended in),

this moment spread out to the
buttery edges of the infinite.

Face reflected back
where there's no one but
    God projecting it.

Silence
    hushed by the

voice of silence.

1/28

## GOD'S BANQUET

Sup at the table of the eloquent
and you'll be drowned in word sauce, with
    condiments from the Latin. And for
dessert, a whipped conundrum served with
    grammatical finesse.
Speak softly, and never be too sure of your
    bearings.

Eat at the table of kings
and you'll be watched very carefully. Speak
    correctly, hold your
        fork just so, don't put your
hands in your lap too much or the
Anti-Assassin guards may have to
        shoot you as you chew.

Have a bite with
    God's own living saints
and the fare may be frugal, the delicacy
    subtle, the silverware made of
        wood or carved stone, the
sweet of such sweetness that actual
dewdrops from heaven are set in globules
    of honey from deep Paradise,

and you'll have to watch the
manners of your heart before the
sweeping glance of the saintly ones
whose smiles in your direction throw
light on years of your true nature and its
daily antics. But

God is Merciful, and His
    saints are only
        doing His bidding at the time of

serving, chewing, swallowing and tasting
all the joys of God's bounty,
all the light thrown out by
    His Presence
to eat by.

Eat directly at God's table
and be at ease,
    be at ease.

The desert may flower before your eyes,
white gazelles may come to watch you
        as you eat,

palm fronds touch the corners of
    your lips with
        delicate touch.

You will be nourished
with almost more than a human can
    bear.

More than a
    human can bear.

1/30

## WINDOWS ONTO THE SOUL

Windows onto the soul, or out of which
  the soul gazes, distracted, daydreaming,
watching the schoolyard with its
  dangling swings, its lengthening
hills beyond the fence, its
  gray sky of always-about-to-rain but
    never pelting.

The window is clear but not smooth, transparent
  but not really flat, not like
most windows which look as if they've been
pressed between two giant iron rollers to
  make the glass so damnably
    flat and even.

These windows are often just chinks in great walls,
slits in foot-thick fortress adobe through which
the convict, if chained to the wall opposite, can
  contemplate either the moat which he
will not cross, or the shark-infested
  ocean he will not enter, those
    razor teeth gnashing just for him.

Some windows, on the other hand, are like those
isinglass affairs in zeppelins, rows of tiny
  rectangles, giving a lovely but
    distorted view of hills and lakes
      passing underneath, clouds and
    snowy peaks.

But windows are also heartbeats.

Each one is a glimpse into beyondness, or
  nearness, or even
    farness,

*plonk* of the moment, *thump* of time,
  *boom* of presentiment, *kaboom* of
joy! Tick of the body clock facing the
true face of the Endless-Time clock,
the window that is there for us
filled with emotion.

The window that is not quite inside us nor
  outside us, that doesn't even
belong to us, but to the Great Window's eternal
  precincts, connects to that endless window of
which ours is like an alotted porthole we can
use for gazing either into or out, each

person of us given one at birth, perhaps the
  only thing we take with us
    when we die, our

singular window reality.

Look, a smudge! Quick,

  the Windex!

2/1

# THE BLIND BEEKEEPER

*for Musa Muhayiuddeen*

**1**

I'd like to make a movie entitled
  "The Blind Beekeeper." Alphonse,
or it could be Henry, blinded by sparks from a
forge when a teenager on his family farm
circa 1943, walks like a man on the moon
(funny how the phrase "man *in* the moon"
  predated the historical event probably by
    centuries) toward his white
wooden bee sanctuaries,

he's wearing no protective suit or headdress,
knows the mental workings of bees,
  can call them individually by
    name, they swarm onto him, if
      that's the right term, they
cover his torso, stripped as he is to the waist,
his face wreathed in smiles,

and he does the dance of the bee with
bees all over him, like a bee pincushion,
this man against a green field on a
    sunny Kansas afternoon, the
      camera rises in a
  spectacular crane shot of Henry
    shrinking smaller and
      smaller, black with
bees, calling each one by name, his

voice on the sound track, each time he
repeats a new name there's an increased
  buzz response, the music of the
soundtrack is a single violin note,

46

the sun's beating down, suddenly there's a
flash of light

and in place of Henry and his bees
there's a large jar of honey, almost white,
as if from Paradise, glowing like a
    pot of gold.

All of this could take place before the
    credits.

Now the story begins.


**2**

We are taken into the bees' world.
Zarzz (all the bees have names starting with
    "Z") has progressive ideas,
he's been to France, feels independent,
    wants to revolutionize the bees'
        lives, thinks about
breaking out of the routine and
    starting his own hive, saves up
pollen secretly in some abandoned
    hexagons in a nearby field,
is in love with Zuzz, wants to
make her his queen.

Zarzz, although commendable on
one level for being a
    bee who wants to make a difference,
doesn't appreciate the divine pattern involved
in being a bee. That there's only
    so far you can go before you
betray beedom, or, potentially tragic in this case,
build, not so much castles in the air, as

hives in hell. But his
   intentions start out as good.

He's in love, he has some thoughts on
improving the lot of bees, but his
   radical ideas might ruin this
hive forever!

Enter the blind beekeeper. He wants to
   learn the higher metaphysics of
bees, to touch with the
   knowledge of his heart the
geometric perfection of the bee, its
almost symbolically ritualistic sets of
   patterns, building patterns, dance
patterns, whose results are
deep medicine for man, prophetically
   ordained, and
the continuation of the species. The

flash he experienced that
   blinded him he wants to
reproduce in the realm of spiritual
   illumination.

Meanwhile Zarzz and Zuzz leave the
   hive in search of
   greener pastures. They pack up their
legs with pollen and head out after
sunset. But bees don't
   fly after dark. They get lost.
They fly into foreign fields. They get
   cold, which is
      fatal for the
      flying mechanism of bees, who
have to keep themselves warm by whirring their
wings. Their story gets quite sad, actually,

and Zarzz suddenly realizes he may have
  doomed both their lives to
    extinction. Being a
thoughtful bee, he is wracked with
guilt and worry, and
starts to pray, for bees are believers,
  as attested to by the beginning of that
word, and have a

beeline to the Divine Reality Who
gave them their wisdom.


**3**

Zarzz: Zee zuzz za za-za-za
  zarzi zuzzo zab zuzzo
    zizz za za-za zarzo zoo.

Zuzz: Zarzi zaz zaz zo-zo-zo-zo-zo
  ziz zar zuzzo zizz zo zo za-za
    zazizzo zazizzo.

Zarzz: Zazo zizo zizz?

Zuzz: Zazo zinzinzup zardo-do zinzanzo
  zar zar.

Zarzz: Zee Zuzz, za zwa zi za zo.


**4**

But the beekeeper is also in love, and he
  also wants to build hexagons of
    perfecton and a palace of
      pure sweetness.

Her name is Rosa, a poor girl from a
   foreign country, and Henry is
her strength and she is his eyes.

But here is the strange part: as Henry
works with the bees, and talks to
   them in their language,
he starts seeing them, *visually*
seeing each one of them. When he's away from their
hive he's blind, but when he faces the
hive he's an alchemist achieving pure gold.

He comes to the hive in the morning.
The hive is in an uproar. He sees them in
clusters talking about Zarzz and Zuzz.
The queen is laying her eggs. The
nurses are taking them to the nursery.
At the center of the hive everything is

   going on as normal. But out in the
streets the bees are literally abuzz.
*"What will we do? What have they
   gone and done? Where could they
have gone? How can we get them back?"*

The blind beekeeper looks into the hive
and sees all this. But suddenly he has
double sight. He sees Zarzz and Zuzz
nearly frozen to death, trying to
sun themselves enough to fly. They are
in a field a few miles away
   bounded by meadow flowers.

There's no time to lose! The beekeeper
calls to the bees. Their round shiny
   multiple eyes all turn to him.
He dances. He dances the dance of

the map to the field they're in.
He turns in circles to indicate miles. He faces
  in their direction. He tilts
   his arms to show the longitude and
    latitude of their
     position.

Now he calls each one by name to
  go to them, to bring them back: "*Go*
*Zuza, Zee, Zan, Zy,*
  *Zarzo, Zeeza, Zanzan, Zink,*
*go Zeno, Zardoz, Zo, Zooey,*
  *Zap, Zeeper, Zazoo, Zip,*
*go Zeezee, Zantham, Zoetrope, Zany,*
  *Zeke, Zap, Zazz, Zoe,*
*Zanzinzo, Zoonzinzan, Zeezay, Zope,*
*go Zaza, Zipe!* They buzz their response!
*Go Zak, z-z-z-z, Zook, z-z-z-z,*
  *Zipper, z-z-z-z, Zay!*

They lift from the hive like an ecstatic
   cloud, they buzz like chainsaws
and off they zoom. The blind
  beekeeper smiles and waves them
   on. Does the story end happily?

They all burst into song!


**5**


Zarzz and Zuzz come back to the hive.
Everyone's glad they're still alive.

The queen makes Zarzz her intimate vizier.
Zuzz marries Zarzz and gets busier and busier.

The blind beekeeper makes lots of money
selling their extraordinary honey

and marries Rosa in a flash of light
so utterly intense he regains his sight.

2/2

# SAVE THE LAST STALLION

Save the last stallion. Put
  glue on its hooves and stick it on the
earth so it won't be sucked
  down into the foam!

Save the sweet tiger's face from
  extinction, that
mask of zigzag lightning, rifts and
cataracts, propulsion in fur, green eyes of
  coherent intelligence,
that the little geologic layers
  of its face not be
rolled up like loose ribbon on the
spool of the end of time.

Save an old mandolin for that high
  plucked note rippling
    back and forth over
a mouth of empty space, that the air not be
  bereft of the sound of
    vibrating strings along with
car horns, crying babies, dripping faucets and
    rain.

Save a line of ants going to and
  from the picnic with
sugary crumbs in their
  mandibles, intent on more than
abstract destinations, toil and sheer
  meandering.

Save a corner of everything, save
every puzzle-piece of the whole, a
tree of each species, one stick insect, one
  stink bug, one glorious

chrysalis of each
    exotic butterfly,

save a hair from the head of every child
to become eyelashes for angels, beads of a
single tear pulling down the
    ends of each one.

Save one of everything in the universe, then let
everything in the universe go, as we

sit transparently in the midst of each
invisible buzzing swarm.

2/7

## CLOUDS

I'd like to write poems that build kind of like
  clouds.
You're in the air and you come upon
  forms in the air that are
mysteriously denser, dark-edged, piled into
  almost bubbling shapes, moving,
majestic, stretched from horizon to horizon,
really expansive and field-like,
wide as the eye can see, and elevated,
rising, shape-changing at faster and
  slower rates,
level upon level, higher and
  higher as from the
window of a plane, then
at a point of peak
it suddenly stretches out to a
  billowing sea of bright light
   below you, froth-horses
charging, silvery, a light so
  bright it's almost blinding, and a
soothing voice or chorus of voices begins to be heard
associated with such lofty elevations.

2/7

# AS FAR AS LIVING IS CONCERNED

As far as living is concerned, some people
  do it better than I do —

I want to ride a
  green horse to the
    center of town, or dial

the Chinese Ambassador on a Wednesday and ask:
  *"Hello, is God palpable to you?*
*Is transparency proof of the existence of Deity*
  *or part of the profound*
    *conundrum?"*

Others, such as my dear wife, are more
conscientiously generous, think all by themselves of
inviting people in, of educating our
  children, while I

dream of building a crystal palace in a tree
  to play xylophones and bells to
    amuse and emancipate the
    neighborhood,

missing a certain earthiness that is a
  required ingredient for
    true saintliness.

2/8

## PIECE OF COAL

The piece of coal that wanted to be diamond
  said to the earth: *Press me.*

The succulent grape that wanted to be wine
  said to the feet: *Crush me.*

The cloud that wanted to be thunder and rain
  said to a facing cloud: *Collide with me.*

The mountain that wanted to be level valley
  said to the elements: *Erode me.*

The oyster that wanted to produce a pearl
  said to a sand-grain: *Irritate me.*

The heart that wanted to be filled with light
  said to the world: *Break me.*

So what's the surprise
at the onslaught, the relentless
avalanche after avalanche of rose petals
  in the form of insurance payments,
natural disasters, arthritis,
    heart trouble and death?
Rose petals big as houses
    propelling through the air at us
like the shields of Hussars
which leave us flat on the battlefield dazed,

but then they assume their

rose petal shapes again
piled in drifts around our
prostrate bodies, so that if our
prostrate bodies are taken away there'll be
the perfect outlines of the absolute
    blessings that have
showered upon us
like the chalk outlines of forensic
    destiny —

O our lives cry out to be pressed to
    diamond, call out to be
crushed to wine, sing out to be made to
fall as merciful rain all around us,

our mountains cry out to be worn down
to passable valleys

so we can fill those valleys
with heart's light

for other travelers
to see by.

2/12

## DREAM QUESTIONS

Only a second ago
  I was having this dream
we were escaping the Aztecs who
  wanted our blood — you know,
up those narrow steps to the top where they
stretch you back on a stone altar,
  tear your heart out with an
obsidian adze — but we were
free, they were coming in hot pursuit,
we had to wait for the sky to darken
then leap out this opening onto flying
gods who would save us —
the sky darkened, I stood on a
  ledge of some sort between
uprights of a wooden structure,
  waited for one of these
wooden gods to fly by. One

flew by, I leaped onto it, grabbed a
wooden strut, it was like a kind of
ancient airplane, all carved and
  painted wood (we had visited a
shop of brightly painted Mexican imports
this evening down on South Street, so
it was like one of those
  large spindly bird figures)
and I stood on its back holding onto the
wooden struts as we flew over the countryside,
saying to it, *"We're escaping those
bloodthirsty Aztecs, they want to*

*sacrifice us, tear our hearts out,"* and the
    bird-god kind of
  looks back at me from its
    flying, I can't quite
describe how, it's a long narrow blue
  bird's head, it turns its eyes to me at the
word "bloodthirsty" as we're
flying over fields in a thunder-darkened
  sky, but

the point is then I woke up. Now I'm
writing this down. Where
was all that? Where did it go?
Will I fall back into it again to
continue the story? Or is
this the continuation, me
getting up, going to the
bathroom, recalling the
dream, deciding to
try to write it down while
  marveling at the whole
wondrousness of its
appearance and disappearance
  just like that!

In the same way that
one moment we're sinning, the next moment
repenting, one moment
glum, the next moment
  rejoicing. One moment
living, the next moment
    dead.

60

Where
does it go? Who

are we now?

2/16

## INTERVIEW WITH A CAT

"OK, what's it like being a cat?"

"Well... we own the house.

We keep to a pretty tight schedule: 8AM:
   the couch; 12PM: the upstairs chair;
   6PM: the floor under the round table.

We barely tolerate your music. We tolerate
your daughter's music. We really dig
your son's rap records.  What does 'yo' mean?

The garbage truck on monday mornings
has got to go. Why don't they just
   pelt the house with rocks?!

We worship the same God.

We're grateful for birds and scratching
   noises.

We love petting.

When we're in power we'll eradicate children.

When everyone leaves the house, you know
we disappear too.  We have our ways...

Now please excuse me -- I have to go
   lie down over there."

# BREAKOUT

*for Doug Froggatt*

As Neruda wrote about being tired of being
   a man,
routine can be a killer!
At 56, taking the black cotton socks off
   every night, sliding down the
underwear, tossing it into the dirty clothes
     box by the door,
getting into the pajamas,

when just one night I'd like to go out and
fell a giant redwood, hear the
   bone-clattering crack of it as it
    falls, its branches
creaking and crashing to the
     ground,

or instead of washing everyone's dishes every night
night after night after a full day's work,
throw them all down a well, a *cenote*, like
  the Aztecs did with their
    pottery every fifty years in
  order to start over from scratch,

instead of getting up every morning in the
  same aging body to stumble like a
   toddler into the
potty to pea
I would slide into day a Masai warrior, my

tall brown body wrapped in a
    dark orange wool cloak as I
    tended my goats in the early morning
      Afric mist,

or instead of driving home the same route
night after night for forty-five minutes through
the same intersections, hoping for
  green lights, jolting to a stop at the
red,
I might actually angle away from the earth
 one night in a kind of pre-Raphaelite
    horse-drawn chariot with
      sunbeams streaming behind me, or
long silver lariats of moonbeams
  as earth recedes smaller than a
     hovering baseball as I

head out into outer space to explore new worlds
where everyone bows and smiles, and the
  fruits from giant fruit trees are also
    giant until they
     fit in your hand when you get
ready to eat them,

but instead I have these moments of
claustrophobic steam-heat heart-freeze,

the same walls, the same
weekly television programs, the
cycles are getting more
tightly wound and seem to

64

come around again quicker,
when there used to be long cycles of Winter and
    Spring and long, long Summers of
white, white porches overlooking the sea in
    wicker furniture, long Summer
    nights with the electric blue
mosquito zapper the only sound in the night,

and a whole lifetime stretched before us
with expeditions to Australia and
    balloon rides over the Himalayas
and laying the intercontinental telegraph line
    and the transatlantic cable,
and writing long heartfelt letters to Victorian
    grandmothers,

but this night of routine is the same night
Moses dwelt in fasting
forty days and nights on Mount Sinai,

and this routine world is the same world
Jesus stood in in the Garden of Gethsemane
at the foot of the Mount of Olives,

and this humdrum earth is the same earth
Muhammad stepped on as he
circumambulated the Kaba in Mecca,

and the angels are here as well as
    elsewhere, bring fresh
messages to our quivering souls
    and take back

brand new
news from us

direct to our Beloved

whose Presence is always near

and nearer,

always nearer and

nearer.

2/19

# ZERO O'CLOCK

At precisely zero o'clock
the seas boil and their
fishes stand on their tails
(they dance to an inner music).

At precisely zero o'clock
the clock on the old clock tower
sighs like a man who's been
oblivious to the
    passage of time and
suddenly realizes it's run out
(it's a sigh that lasts for
    a hundred years).

At precisely zero o'clock
    zebras change stripes,
what's zigzag black becomes
zigzag white, but only a
few bluebottle flies
    notice the difference
(they get faces of the local
constabulary and land on donuts).

At precisely zero o'clock
the ocean waves turn to linoleum
and ducks wear large basketball
    sneakers to maneuver the
    curves and dips
(they quack in rhythm and sound like a
    jubilant crowd).

At precisely zero o'clock
the maiden loses her virginity
   to a higher power
and gains the virginity of
never having a thought enter her
that isn't a divine thought
(now she sings like an angel).

At precisely zero o'clock
the face you have loved all these
   years turns like a
sunflower to the source of
   sunlight and its
petals become dazzling
while the inside face remains
somewhat recognizable
(its eyes dance merrily
 and its lips pucker).

At precisely zero o'clock
we all become pure spirit and
take each other by the
   hand and walk like
wind under a door
to a place of perfect peace
(there's never been anything like it!
Wait till you taste it!).

2/21

## CONCEPTION

Teeny-tiny people, about the
   size of your thumbnail,
walk around on the earth, and when they
    catch a glimpse of us
they take us for their god — we can
do things like put ladders up against a
   wall, set things on fire,
      walk across puddles.

Now let's hope we don't do the same thing,
let's hope this isn't what happens in our
   own theology, some
     imaginary giant
beings glimpsed from their dimension, just
an elbow or toe, attributed with
  divine powers and miraculous
    abilities, the
next dimension up, peopled with
normal people just like us, going about their
business, occasionally
   popping into our dimension
to carry out some display of divine
  miraculousness, like
vacuuming the floor,
   opening a window,
killing a rat.

Michaelangelo has God
leaning forward on a cloud, finger extended,
a magnificent being to be sure,

majestic as an old Italian actor
who's aged well, but

God?

It's not so cartoon-like. It's more
harrowing and wonderful, mysterious,
    invisible.

The outside day is filled with sunlight.

Cheeping birdsong can be heard.

2/22

70

## SAND BLOWN AWAY

Sand blown away from the giant face, grain by
   grain, to reveal
not the great reclining Nile Flood God Washtup
   but Sam Hohotep, seller of those
    little vials of Egyptian glass
     you put perfume in.

The sunken treasure lifted to the surface,
   waves receding and washing around it,
to reveal not the
   famous pirate Richard Badass's
much-rumored chest of pillaged trinkets
but his overnight bag filled with
12 freshly laundered ruffled shirts, pig-bristle
   toothbrush, and
 2 pairs of newly polished shoes,
    brass buckles still gleaming.

The personal diary of the great philosopher Loquacious,
   dug up from his
    powdery clutter, his tiny Latin
handwriting deciphered, to yield a
   litany of petty complaints and grudges,
as well as spews of obscenity he'd
    never have let himself employ
     in his thousands of
"classical" pages.

Often the "glory that was" becomes instead
various blueprints for an outhouse,

a medicinal recipe for indigestion, purloined
love letters for
  an adultery. A live banquet for the dead.

And the great conspiracies become instead
little insidious vendettas
  against someone's presumed
    power,
when no one really

has any.

## TWO LINES WRITTEN DURING
## A PERFORMANCE OF OLIVIER
## MESSIAEN'S TARANGULILA SYMPHONY

Surrealism takes as much of a man as possible.

A bone is more than a month and three sisters.

3/1

# SINGING

*To my wife on our 17th wedding anniversary*

**1**

Over the distant marsh, across reed beds
  where geese are nesting,
    you can hear singing.

Out the downtrodden neighborhood window,
  across the rotted wooden windowframe,
you can hear singing.

From between the loud metallic steaming
  railroad trains in the railroad station,
    in an overcast
gunmetal gray afternoon, clouds on
top of each other, you can hear singing.

From the house in the middle of a field,
grass peaked roof, cows meandering down a
  bright green hillside,
    you can hear singing.

Down a really dark street in Shanghai, between
  shouts and sing-song cries, smells of
    sesame oil,
      you can hear singing.

At the end of a long road, Himalayan
  shadows where vultures circle

looking for a dead meal,
  you can hear singing.

Out at sea, from a sudden rowboat
  caught between troughs of water,
in the literal middle of nowhere,
    you can hear someone
      singing a poignant
wordless melody
to no one in particular, linking up
with the sly aborigine in cowboy levis
suddenly going primitive in downtown
  Sydney on a bus, by singing,

or rainforest dweller waiting for the
poison from his dart to set in
on the treetop monkey, passes the
  time by singing a
    one syllable song
      over and over,

and the crooner in the white spotlight
aboard a luxury steamer, late at
night, most people drunk, but
as he takes the microphone in the
full moon far out from any shore
suddenly everyone's sober and suddenly
  thoughtful about their mortality
and look across at each other
as the has-been crooner starts singing,

and the naked boy with the long stick

on top of the water buffalo trying to
get it to cross the mud puddle they're in
who decides to wait for the
  beast to decide for itself, and
    so begins singing,

and this late night song of mine as almost everyone's
asleep, it's two-thirty in the
ante meridiem morning, my mouth is
shut, there's absolute
  silence except this
    world in words that's
opened up to my
      inner singing,

but the song opens out, it gets
louder and louder as the good earth turns in the
night and somewhere people wake up,
songs in their heads, get up to
  wash faces and shave and

notice they're singing, get as
naked as the day they were
born into a shower and put on the water
  full blast and find they're
belting out a song, and it

builds in momentum and sound, it
lights up the sky, the
  simple, exorbitantly
    gorgeous
sound of divinely inspired

(as everything else is!)

    singing.


**2**


The song is a blurt, a bleep, a
    song in a ditch,
a fly, a fuzz of fur in the
    air, a glint of light,
it's airborne, underwater, earthbound,
    over the top,
lighter than air, longer than air,
    a simple air,
air in the lungs, light in the lungs
    laughter, it's
clink of glasses, clunk of marble tabletops
    touching, clank of the
prison door,
    Clark Kent changing, that's it, it's
caterpillars pulling out their
    extended wings and
flying, youth turning into age
    and still managing to sing,
youth turning back into youth and
    singing, it's a
plane taking off, a blimp landing, a
    bicycle going down a hill,
wind in the hair, skating down a hill,
    water current pulling,

undertow, tip-toe, do-si-do,
all of these and none,
the song is everything and
nothing
sung by God,
we live and die along its
rise and fall,
melody rising, melody falling,
  the song is alone,
the notes are dots of light in the
  endless night.
Night-night, night-owl, turn out the
  night-light.
Song of light lit like another
  star in the night.
Echo of song a galaxy sings
out in the night.

We sing the song for a while
and then we are light.

3/7

## BRIDGE

There's a bridge in space we would
    all walk on if we could
since it confers conscious insight on the viewer
of everything that crosses its path

and every whisper that crosses the heart

and every thought stream that bifurcates from the
main source into two contradictory
    sluices both vying for
      supremacy.

This bridge (I almost hesitate to
    call it a bridge, yet it
      does span where
one place drops off and another begins)
is also its own time zone,
geese flying through it seem almost to be
    flying backwards,
in the rush of water that flows beneath the
bridge the ripples of the current
    seem almost to have stopped
      and formed dunes.

There is a certain music no human
    instrument produces,
it has become one of the components of
    time and space, a dimension
      unto itself. It

strikes a constant sympathetic
chord inside the heart.

It is the starting point for the
  growth of great forests, the
excavation of the great seas with all their
    arcane undersea life
as well as the vivacity on the lips of every
    air-breathing creature.

This music is the dimension
architecturally charted and
extended by the composition of
poems. With each new poem
guided from its opening of inspiration
    to its closing chord
another "room in space" of tangible sound
is added onto the
interior construction of the universe.
(It has always existed — it is
  newly minted, as if opening
rooms after winter in a
Russian dacha, removing
  white sheets from the furniture, bringing
life to rooms again after cold disuse).

And as we
  stride on this bridge, waving
goodbye to old thoughts, friends, connections,
    associations, zoological
  Latin names of birds, precious stones,
    loved ones, a spray of

vision blows against us
and in each droplet is a world, on the

surface is ourselves acclimatizing
to a visionary universe, while
in the depths of each drop
lie the mysterious evolutions of
  all things through their
dramatic upheavals and
   cascading reversals

to a blue sky with geese flying
through it going in time as fast as it
  takes grains of sand to
    form, or light to
fall on us from a
distant galaxy, or the
ripples of water currents
  to seem to come to a
stop and form dunes. And this

bridge in space we would
walk on if we could is the
bridge in space we do
walk on in space and time as we
attend, in each moment, the

atomic wedding
of heartbeat to heartbeat and

breath to breath

our gaze
returning again to us
from the interior heart of
another

   to our own
   face from the

Face of God.

3/11

# MY DAUGHTER

*for Salihah*

My daughter sits very still on the
petal of a camelia on the
waters of a small shaded pond.

She is fifteen going on sixteen

shaped like a young Mongolian horse
with flying mane and full flying tail.

Her heart is the scherzo of a particularly
    moving trio by Beethoven played on
        glass instruments.

The world is beckoning to her like the smoky
        post-midnight part of a
particularly honky-tonk port city with
    snaky neon signs and snare drums,
and her ears, like the new wet wings of
        tropical butterflies,
flutter slightly and appear about to
    detach themselves and fly in the
        direction of the sound, but
remain instead on the sides of her head
fanning slowly back and forth in the sunlight
        to dry.

Her heart is an entire forest of streams and
    underground water basins,

a very beautiful and serene primitive
    tribe lives on the banks of its
        rivers who have no word for
"hatred" or "warfare" and who
    smile with flashing teeth
            and give up their hammocks
            to each new visitor.

Her heart is a long moonlit stairway in somewhere like
    Vienna, stone lions on pedestals
        protecting it.

It is a very beloved place to God, her heart,

a place of small pleasure boats and
echoing laughter over splashing water.

Her heart is new and cries out, protects her
vulnerable friends and her friends'
    vulnerabilities and often forgets
        her own.

She is a very beautiful white mythical
    galloping animal on the
        rim of the ocean, small
hooves beating green foam.

My daughter is a grown girl and a
newly formed woman.

Her long dark hair belongs to the
natives of far Pacific Islands.

Her eyes belong to herself and see through
    long dark lashes
that easily fill with tears, my daughter,
my own flesh and blood, she is

a new continent over a dark
unexplored area of the globe,

but the music we already hear from the
villagers is naturally rhythmic

and played on sweet instruments.

My daughter is one of God's sweet instruments
playing slow scales in a shaft of
burnished sunlight, flute-like and bright,

trying out melodies in this life
never quite played before

but as ancient as rain.

3/12

## THE HEART IS A WHITE BOWL

The heart is a white bowl of fresh
  sweet peaches set in the
windowsill in the sunlight.

The head is a slow nod
in the direction of Truth.

The body is a highway in a
Third World country in
constant need of repair.

The soul is an endless measure of moonlight.

The soul is a white spot in a black field.

The soul is a black spot in a white field.

The soul is a green estuary in a
  shadowy area.

I stand up inside the
shadow of the soul.

I look out through the eyes of
  no one.

The seeing is God's.

What is seen by His Seeing
is visible proof of His existence.

The sunlight the white
bowl of fresh peaches sits in.

The white bowl of peaches,

and the ray of yellow sunlight in which
the white bowl of sweet peaches sits.

3/19

## VARIOUS SAINTS

Saint Ignazio Cortez Mendoza de Vadilla turned in his
   cell to watch his
      crucifix burst into flame then sparkle into
glorious love-scattering light on his
      wall.

Lester Elderman Croft shifted in his chair
because his dinner suddenly became
a host of angels singing *Hosanna! Hosanna!*

Carol Lederbach Hecht squinted her eyes at the
blackboard as she wrote today's
Latin lesson for the children waiting in their seats
      for the letters were suddenly stars
         singing in a windy heaven.

T. Hunter Hunter let his jaw drop visibly as the
haltered and cinched expedition reached the
      South Pole to see
a multitude of naked human-like creatures doing a
dance in innumerable interlocking circles,
      some wing'd, some not,
         around an invisible point.

Raul Soap depressed the brake pedal
   of his full bus of retired folk
to let the halo'd herd of misty elephants
cross the street at Parsifal and Pine.

Audrey Bentham Patterbun Scott

let out a gasp as she saw the
reflection in the soupspoon she held
in front of her face
was not of herself but of Queen Elizabeth I
powdered and pink in her giant lace collar
sitting stiff and opening her eyes,
      mouthing the words
            over and over: *Noblesse Oblige.*

Ralph (pronounced Rafe) Stoddard Jr.
smiled as he leaned over the railing of the
sloshing tuna boat to watch
strings of light spell out
      enigmatic sentences in the
            air above the dark and
                  dusky waves,
            accompanied by a
                  sense of general wellbeing.

And so it goes on our planet, wherever
there are eyes and hearts,
phenomena keep leaping into
      hyper-space and
            back again as if
it were the most
natural thing for them to do.

Angels lean down from their
places and touch
tips of things with their wings.

I salute the light in the air, and I also
     salute the air!

I draw a little bit of it in to make
new shapes in my lungs, entering
     the blood and spreading
out through tiny capillaries to my skin,

and then I let a little bit back out again,

     and this in itself
is wonder enough, one
     person on the planet among
plenitudes practicing this
miraculous magic, like an alchemical

     expert on light, like a

     master engineer of air!

                            3/22

## SICK IN BED

Sick in bed,
I don't want to turn on the news.
I want to
  shut my eyes and
turn my head to the wall.

I don't want to know if some
Palestinians were shot,
if a Russian leader threatens war.

I want to imagine I'm a huge
  dragonfly
hovering over a pond.

3/23

## MOOSE TRAINS

Moose trains. The idea that
boxcars filled with moose are
  clacking along tracks, taking them
to a moose paradise somewhere, those
ugly horse faces and architecturally
  ungainly antlers, monstrous and
    majestic creatures (how do they
sleep? Heads on hooves in a
  forest clearing big enough for those
chandeliers of horns to clear? How do they
  get through thickets, that
    Star Wars assemblage on their
horsey heads getting stuck between
  branches?) Well,

*Moose trains.* Or maybe, more humanely,
meaning an annual
  migration of moose, a loose
single file parade of moose through the woods
going north or south to where
moose are most content to just be
moose. Moose *Trails*. Pines and cedar trees
filtering sunlight down on
  a long line of migrating moose.

"Moose Trains."  The two words
  came to me on the
way to the bathroom and I saw a
kind of personal poetic testament
of angular rhapsody, long horizontal lines

92

taking in our modern world and its
apparent farewell to the
  ancient natural one, I thought of
trains filled with forlorn moose going
slowly along through their
natural habitats, Canadian forests, Northern Wyoming,
wherever they roam, getting rid of these
larger-than-life seemingly prehistoric
relics of a forest life that's gone
  almost entirely interior, the
scary psychic forests where sudden
  screams chill the bone, and the
apparition of moose might suggest a
   really horrible reality.

Those tall dark heads with extended
lips and veritable tree boughs of
headpieces, swaggering
  out of the
   night. Like that

nightmare painting by Blake's friend
  Fuseli, with the
ghost-eyed horse's head looming ecstatically
   out of the dark.

I hear a far-off forlorn train whistle,
  a forlorn train horn echoing between
snowy hills as the train in the cleft below
with its boxcars filled with standing
  stomping moose winds endlessly
along, their moosey brains

bewildered at why they're being
carried along.

Moose trains.

Like a slow, sad song.

3/24

## I CAN'T SLEEP

I can't sleep.
I'll have to saddle up the black horse
   with the silver-white head
and ride backwards through time
until I come to Radsforth manor
   on the hill and go in and
court Emily Dickinson, who will
      reject me, for I do not
         buzz loud enough in her
      empty room, I do not
watch through half lids the
   landlocked martyr of rainbows
saw through the ditch.

And so I will go from Radsforth manor
and walk for a few years back through time over
   hill and dale planting
apple trees until the plainsfolk
      call me crazy while their
         children listen to my tales
      and the girls patch my jacket
and the boys want to come with me
but I go off every morning

back through time
on board a large and ghostly ship
   swarmed aboard in the China Sea by
Malay pirates with gleaming teeth and
      impeccable manners who
retain in their company those with a

spirit of adventure and able bodies enough to
brave ragged storms and the
    taking of Spanish fleets,
cannon and musket shots
ringing in my ears

as I lie on a hot beach near the
beginning of time wondering if the
booms are from man's cruelty to man
or the formation of planets,
God's cosmic plan detonated on the
vast field of space, my

body wracked with exhaustion
naked as a mountaintop,
head resting on my
arms, hoping to fall

    asleep.

3/25

# EDGES

I glimpsed the possibility (in my mind's
   half-shut eye at least) of
pulling away from the cutting
   edges of things in this world, of
edges generally, of pulling away from them, I
     say, in such a way that
one falls into the spatial gulf that
comes only at the meeting point of
   edges. Huge shapes in space, pulling an
object from its surrounding space in such a way that
one is liberated from the body into
buoyant spaciousness, totality and
completeness, our

bodies above all, even the hand with its
curved fifty-seven-
   year old five fingers I use to
write this, and even the
pen point on paper dragging the liquid
   asphalt of black ink out in peculiar
    handwriting to write the
articulation of it down.

The table my elbow rests on, say we
glance back from its edge, and instead of just
falling down onto the floor at our feet
we suddenly were present at a
sheer arctic edge of clear blue glacier ice
in the brilliant shine of northern daylight
with huge movements of land mass and

sky cloud, huge
  underground movements of
    seismic shifts and
      whale bulk, crying

terns overhead, long white
  wingspread in tight
    coils in the
air overhead,

or glanced away to the right from the
edge of a tall black vase full of
  early spring daffodils on the
    table where I write and

suddenly we're in a street in Victorian
  England, brick walls and
staircases, horse-hoof clop and
  carriage-creak, shouts of
schoolboys and bell-tinkle,

away from the innocuous edge of a
  bud vase into a sidereal universe
    of encapsuled
time and space, that by

going from the knife edge of this
life as we perceive it we are
whooshed into the world of spirit,
  clunk of planks over an abyss,
clank of chains of being and chains of
  non-being, broken, shackles

98

shaken off, we pull back in
profile, the whole world opens up in the,
not the shadow, it's not a
   matter of shadow, not even of
light, but

what's there when the edge is pulled away,
ocean-liner prow, cliff-edge, knife-edge, sharp
   edge of
 thought, or the touching edges of two
      thoughts in agreement,
body edges touching, electrical, alive,

the electrified edges of Kirilian
   photographs of things,
chasms of energy down which the
Voice of God can be heard, thunderously
sweet and intimate Creator,
Consoler and Illuminator of everything,

eyelid's edge closed over eyes,
sharp wind-chime sound in the wind outside,
even furry edge of refrigerator hum in this
room where I write, pull it

away and we're in the land of super-
   spectacular singing, primordial
waterworld, elemental
   concordance of the aurora borealis
shivering through everything, whisper whose
edge is intimate words in the
heart, edge pulled away and we're all the

way from the oral fixations in epic
   proportions of Homer blind on the
edges of the battlefields of his mind

to the slithering sound of the vibrations of one
violin string alone in a sound so
   silent, a room so

silent there's no

sound.

## SURROUNDED BY RAIN

I can't imagine worshipping God in
    ancient Egypt, with steaming
        libations offered between Anubis
pillars by slender virgins of both
    sexes on silver and gold platters
to the plucking of plectrums, with the
sacrifice of new lambs and the
archaic invocations of hunchbacked priests
in steaming hot temples to the
lapping sound of nearby Nile and the
occasional screech of ibis,

or the worship of God in
    Aztec America with feather-caped
priests (and not even
    necessarily on heart-sacrifice day)
climbing the almost
    vertical staircase to the Sun Temple
to offer, with appropriate chants and at
appropriate conjunctions of
    planets and moon, whatever was
appropriate to offer,
supplicant down below, the priest
way up there, wreathed in green incense mist,
saying whatever and with
    whatever look on his face,

or worshipping God in a great
draughty medieval cathedral
behind black-cloaked processions of

censor-swinging monks singing
plainchant with exalted
     crisscross of voices and interwove
themes, the priest on the ornate
     altar elevating the host,
the aromatic smoke of frankincense and
     myrrh overwhelming someone kneeling on
cold stones, hearing
     angels' wings flapping
     ever-so-softly in the
distant darkness of nave and
     echoing arch,

but rather to be as purely elegant as
waking just after dawn, the
     rain kerplunking outside,
washing face and arms and
     feet with fresh
cold water, laying the prayer mat
     down, its front edge toward
          Makkah, standing directly before

God and raising hands to the
     sides of the head to
begin the prayer and then
quietly beginning it,

speaking the Arabic of the Beloved
     Prophet, word for word, on
one's own lips, heart like a
     suspended
     stillness within a

stillness, going to
one's knees before Him and putting
forehead on ground before
His Might and Majesty
alone in one's room,

in the silence of morning
surrounded by a watery
trickle of rain.

3/26

## THERE WAS NO SOUND

The blind girl moved through the night
  like a gliding bird,
her heart sang the map of her
   momentary destination:
  *"Turn right, go a hundred paces."*
The world as measurement appeared before
   her inner eyes. She was
geometrician of twilight.
Wisdom outlined her. Made her
  senses like neon.
She sang the world into being
  that was sung within her.

Then the sky stopped (there was
   a chunk sound)
and we were in the Land of Transformations.

The girl was changed into a
  soft white goose.

We walked down to the stream to see
where the Land of Transformations began.

My pen became a feather

and there was no sound.

## DEATHBED POEM

I want to write a deathbed poem
on my deathbed.

I say this sitting on the side of my
bed before sleep
not knowing, when I finally
   sidle down to lie down
whether it will be my deathbed
or not. So I

want to write a last poem
worthy of a deathbed utterance or
realization, not as a
  practice, since you
    really can't practice your
death experience the way you might
practice, say, a birth class, hunkering
down and deep breathing, yet

in fact we can practice our
death and say
  farewell from the actual
edges of ourselves to the retracting
   edges of the universe,
and horizontalize on the slow
  barge, drifting
Chinese fortune-cookie ticker-tape goodbyes
    behind us, illuminated
moments so concave with exuberant
  light they might contain a

life, or an
illuminating glimpse of life, or life
    itself, the life of
death. And

tonight when 38 members of the Heaven's Gate cult
were found suicided in San Diego, immaculately
dressed, with five dollar bills in their
    pockets, tote bags packed for an
        extraterrestrial out-of-body
            trip away from earth and all its
boundaries, frozen in a kind of
    metaphysical refrigerator
stretched out on bunk beds under
    triangular purple shrouds,
— no deathbed poems there! —
some clutching the
recipe for a potent mixture of Phenobarbital,
    vodka and vanilla pudding, a final
farewell toast to end all toasts —

and yet when we lie down, fully intending to get
    up still alive tomorrow,
we don't know what magnitudes of celestial
    rapids might intervene, what
divine Niagaras, down

which, without barrels, we might roll!

Or crossing a street, or standing quite
still in one place (a fiery piano
    falling on us from above, an

inflamed ventricle falling on us from
    within),

so each utterance should perhaps have
a hillside with a sunny disposition,
a snowfall of light on a barn roof
  speckling it with starlight, or

a black inviting room as warm as
mother breast, father beard,

a whole cave of human understanding and
    longing, a few pithy lines
      scratched in the
      wall before we leave,

some dramatic gesture!

When it's really just the backs of innumerable
sheep, docile in late afternoon sun, scarlet
    light streaking their wool, their

benign almost human faces, facing

nightward.

3/27

## LEGACY

If I leave as my legacy a certain smile
stashed up on rocks by delirious sea birds,
or the way I counted on my ten fingers
wiggling in the air with alternative wiggles,
or inflected my questions up at the end,
or started high and ended low,
or wore cotton socks of a shocking blue
with otherwise ultra-conservative clothes,
or sang after midnight if I thought I could
or tap-danced on thin ice in my stocking feet,
or recited the names of the stars in pig Latin,
or went out after noon without a hat,
if I thought that any or all of these things
might be good or eternal enough to last
for future generations, the twitch in my cheek,
the cluck of my tongue, the wink of my eye,
the way I stutter when I'm asking for money,
the way I yell if I'm forced to lie,
the way I stumble as I leave the stadium
after the believers have been eaten by lions,
the way I lean out over the railing
thinking I see in the frothing waves
a perfect emerald City of Light,
   or deep Neptunian
    caverns of darkness,
if any of these things survive my life
it'll be like an echo that makes an arch
over canyon cascades of the wildest waters
hitting the canyon walls like ice
that falls in a glass to melt away

the way gestures vanish as soon as they're made,

or names get forgotten from our earliest memories,

or animals fall asleep at the zoo

when nobody's looking.

4/2

# TWA FLIGHT TO SIOUX FALLS

Up among clouds
  I become a more definite self —
notice my gestures of impatience, discomfort,
  tension or tiredness in my eyes,
anxious about hovering in midair while
    moving forward above the
  multicolored parquet of
    Midwest fields below,

anxious about falling out of the sky,
anxious about landing and what
  awaits me, but also

a penguin island of dully lit heart-space where
I cling to the Inevitable
and buoyant hope in God, keeping God's
Name subvocally going in case His
  invisible realm suddenly
    claim us and we
whoosh out of this world like
flies out of a bottle, or like

gorgeously illuminated souls arrayed in a
  blinding sudden nakedness,

flying to our Source.

4/3

110

## THE STATE IN WHICH EVERYTHING
## IS PERFECT

The state in which
  everything on earth is
    perfect as it is.
(Oh the agony, the agony of it,
and the sweetness!)

I walked by a student dorm at night and a
  girl in T-shirt and levis was talking on a
    remote phone on the balcony
with love sounds and half-giggles, and I
saw her youth and joy and my
      heart rose up to heaven.

Then I entered the motel lobby where I was staying
and a young, fleshy Sioux Indian boy was
looking for the
night clerk to get a room, and I flashed on the
agony of his tribe. And yet

the state in which everything on earth is
perfect as it is, the love, the agony,
sweet words from the heart, a
  killing blow to the
head, sad births, happy deaths,
this planet among its starry neighbors
  circulating in space here
bathing in malevolence and beneficence
yet never singing off-key — the ocean waters
never just getting into a boat and

paddling off without
  crashing back on the rocks,

the hand lifted to strike a wife either
held in the air or coming
  down with brute force, how can
this be perfection? A
child born hooked on drugs in its
  incubator, how can its

poor days be
    called perfect?

The love I feel toward your eye as well as
the mote in your eye — but

could I sing in a tyrant's chains?
Could my battered body under constant torture
    still house a
  peaceful rose garden where I might
circulate like the unperturbed earth
  among the strong and weak
    rosebushes lifting
perfect aphids off of perfect leaves,
  my heartbeats as steady as
    ocean waves returning
      to shore?

Yet God is Perfection, and the
wind can't turn at right angles,
though it spiral and loop in sometimes
  ever-widening circles.

112

Does the person flying through the
    air to his death
sing a glory chorus from
        the ultimate canticle?

Arms spread out or not, mouth
wrenched in a scream, or singing?

Eyes open or closed
to the sweetness and
    agony of

perfection?

4/3

113

# ALLEN GINSBERG DEAD AT 70

## 1

An old bear shambles to his death.

I don't know why I've taken an
  image out of nature to
    commemorate Allen Ginsberg's death, the
quintessential New York poet, bear-man of
our anguished human heart.
Bear man. Hair wild, ecstatic finger-cymbal
  singing, bear-voiced true bard of our
century, serene somehow at the
center of it. Something

bear-like, a small bear, physically shrunken in his
  late 60's, whereas in the
1960's he was an
  unstoppable dynamo. Hair-raising
roof-raiser of consciousness, fleshy
  permission-giver of nature's
orgasmic flow, wild arm'd and
hoarse-voiced grizzly of
    poetry!

Died, I heard today on TV in a
Day's Inn Motel room in Sioux Falls, South Dakota,
  having, like him, come to read poetry
    and talk to youth,
and where I actually thought of him this morning
passing through so many hotel rooms in this world on his

indefatigable poetry odyssey, Czechoslovakia,
   China, Berlin, Bombay,
exciting us to the Light of God even when he
   denied Him, the cosmic
vibrations and cataclysmic
   harmonies of this human and
inhuman universe we find ourselves in.

The hydrogen jukebox has gone dim.

Cancer finally defeating him.

Old bear shambling in a dark part of the
   forest, inspecting an acorn in his
      giant paw, licking with that
         purply tongue,

huge bulk gone into the dark

to learn the Truth
      at last!


**2**


A land of crystalline bridges,
   so gorgeous it makes you gasp,
where rainbows are almost circular,
   lakes like smooth glass.

Herons leap in the air, then open their
   wings.

Insects suspend themselves like
  vibrating violin strings.

Light seems to be multi-pointed,
    shimmering in the
  air, tubular columns of
    incandescence rising everywhere.

Arches of mist we walk through, entering
  another world.

Corridors of mountainous landscapes
  like a screen unfurled.


**3**


Allen, on the same TV in the same motel room
  I found out about your death
Dr. Quinn in her outwest frontier town
treated tall bewhiskered Walt Whitman for
  stroke and the whole town turned out to
greet the famous poet with love and respect until
some people thought his poems obscene and
gossip was he "loved the company of men."

Lots of Whitman's poetry was heard, rare for
  a television drama,
and all was resolved when he recited
*Song of Myself* in an open meadow
to a handful of people sitting in the
  middle of a mass of empty chairs.

116

**4**

The airplane jostles through the air,
  wind blows it around.

Bumps in the sky road, while
outside the window flashes pure sky.

White sky, snow-blank, way up here
  above earth on my
   way back from
South Dakota to Philly.

Sky all around — if we
pushed past earth's gravity we could
just keep going into sky! We'd need

thrusters, rocket fuel, massive intensity
to break past earth's iron belt.

Then would we be
  free?

The *Tibetan Book of the Dead*, to avoid
  reincarnation, commands the
recently deceased, whose
  hearing is still intact, to hold to the
Great White Light, and not
   flinch. That

embrace of Light keeps the soul from
falling back into matter, it says,

assuming Original Enlightenment,
  finally becoming light.

Your heart was worn and tattered, Allen,
  so spent on love, and the
mill wheels of love, grinding, grinding.

We loved you while you were here.
You were a noble companion.

Hold to the light.

4/6

118

## CAN'T HELP IT

There's no reason to believe
that because the floor is relatively
solid underfoot (it doesn't sway like
   alligator's back or dolphin's),
the walls more or less
solid (I haven't tried
walking through them lately, afraid of
  banging nose and
    toes if I did),
my life fairly simple (I
turn a mill wheel with the
other donkeys, drop off and
pick up teenage daughter and her
  friends ever-giggling),
enjoy the company of wife
(even though her loving patience with me
  as I am sometimes
seems the height of absurdity),
the countryside seems relatively at
peace (no robber-bands or
Kalashnikov-wielding rebels
  ambush car on way or
from work, commandeering its
  use to barrage
   sandbag barricades and
kidnap the mayor or any of his many superiors or
    subordinates),
the world itself seems to be
rotating as normal (a few floods, earthquakes,
  volcanic eruptions or

reports of the sky falling
notwithstanding),

there's just no reason to believe that
because all these things are running along
    somewhat in order that
this is the way things are, that

the waves of the sea do not hide
Neptune's court of oceanic djinn who
ride giant seahorses and all
    sport tridents in the manner of their
master, that

clouds in the sky do not hide
legions of angels as thick as
    fireflies moving in
choric sheets of song and
    brilliant light down from
        heights so ethereal their
faces are beatified by the recent glare of
divine perfection and their
wings multiplied a thousand-fold
in vibratory precision,

that each space our bodies traverse
isn't wider and deeper than the oceans that
surround us, higher than skyscrapers,

or that snow-capped Kilimanjaro peaks
from our feet to our heads are
worlds of time and space so

opposite to this one that
spectacular histories of giant and pygmy
nations come to
    birth and pass in the
        blink of our
two (or more)
    eyes (depending),

nothing is as it seems,

and yet
the sweet world in repose, the countryside
more or less grandmotherly, my
life with its hectic routines and small
    pay, my cherished wife and
children, this nighttime and
    daytime house of reality whose
outdoor and indoor rooms I
        pass through under the
constant gaze of God Whose Mercy I depend on
is all camouflage more than worthy of my affections,
a kiss on my brow from it from
        time to time in
exchange for a
kiss or two on its naked
cheek from me, with always a

consecutive heartbeat kept for the true Owner of it all
and a knowing wink to indicate we

know we're actually
fooling each other, the world and

I, but

it's a visceral agreement between us.

In fact we

can't
help it!

4/13

## COBALT BLUE

Cobalt blue! Whose
very name alone would
make me a believer, but whose
color in transparent glass
against light from a window

lifts the mind to a fantasy of
deep darkness, of
sea-depths, undersides of
sunken hulls, treasure,
deepsea tropical caverns,
night. But

night with a holy radiance,
cloisters, Mediterranean
monasteries, Greek
bottles on high walls overlooking
the brighter blue sea —

*cobalt blue glass!*

Shadowy translucence!

Sexual celestial!

During the day:
  *night!*

4/13

## PIANO OF THE NIGHT

There's an old piano up above that calls itself
The Piano of the Night. It plays some
   funky tunes. It plays a
slow rag. It plays what crickets on
   lilypads in black pools can hardly
sing. It

stays there on the low wall of the clouds
and plays twelve-arm'd music to make a thousand
tiny seahorse babies curl their
    tails around tendrils deep
       undersea.
Chords struck that sound twelve-handed
make redwoods shoot up, their
   crowns coronating heaven.
Much finger exercise up and down the keys
keeps trains running
   more or less on schedule, lips
making contact with other lips, heartbeats
skipping a beat from time to time to make
regular heart rhythm vastly more intriguing,

The Piano of the Night. In a tall
   hall. Surrounded by
slender figures in floor-length gowns
holding fronds. Luminous.
A distant music can be heard. As of

distant hooves getting closer. This

was meant to be a tightly-knit
heart-rending poem with large
harmonies. Like my thoughts at the

moment, large independently floating
islands of sound (crashing chords, surf)
and meaning (the cocked ear hears
majestic silences down through which
meanings go in search of meanings.

And out of which
meanings upon meanings emerge).

4/18

## TALKING TO GOD

I'm Mr. Goof
and You're Divine Speech.
I can
come to You,
and Your river keeps flowing.

I'm Mr. Far
and You're Near.

If my duck's feet get stuck
   in a bucket
You'll release me,
and if I've
   dived into Your Lake, You'll
release me from
various mistaken identities, lost
green passports to Nowhere, upset
stomachs from eating
   empty space, mental
indigestion from too many busy pictures,
      mortal fatigue.

The wonder is we know You at all!

Behind every rushing
cascade, every towering and hallowed
   redwood, every screaming
tornado, every change of season,
indications of Your
            Great Presence,

and a deep desire on our part to
know Your most intimate Name.

You've been called so many things,
but if we call on You at all,
   You're Near,

and if we lean forward or actually
   come toward You,
Your Divine Presence presses around us
like a night of great luxury
   after dwelling too long
    in cardboard houses,

or daylight streaming
especially for us
from a blanket of darkness
thrown over the face of heaven.

In every lifetime,
You've never lied.

Your Beneficent Patience with
the thousand implausible stories we tell You
one right after the other, without
letup, like faucets left on in
   satanic palaces,
    amazes me.

But the night is long,
and Your Generosity knows no bounds.

We always walk away
with a newborn lamb in our arms

and a heart full of roses.

4/22

## ALL THE PLACES I MAY NEVER VISIT

I think of all the places I may never
   visit before I die
and all the things I may never see,

the Taj Mahal with its filigree, its
echo I've been told reverberates farther than
reverie, its reflection as if
   suspended on cloud in the long
perpendicular pool at its base,
    screaming peacocks in its cinnamon trees,
serene Bengal tigers at its gates,
jungle roads with fakirs fulfilling their
   yogic vows, one hand held aloft for
all eternity. I

probably won't get to India, for all its
beauty and poverty.

Nor probably China either, though I've two
young friends who've made the trip and one
was inspired as well as awed by
bicycles, bicycles, bicycles, and Chinese people
everywhere, Chinese spoken, Chinese
written, nothing like it,
he and his father white sore thumbs in a crowd,
and what a crowd! I

probably will miss the Hidden City, Forbidden
City, hub of the world, gate behind
wall behind gate, everything interlocked, screens and

shadowy halls, ivory latticework and gold dragon
cloisonné, blue jackets, blue jackets, blue
caps and more blue
    jackets, streets almost
steamy with noise and bustle, the Great Hall my
    19 year old friend said even he huffed and
        puffed to see,

nor Tibet I'd love to see,
under the inscrutable Chinese boot,
the love I had for it in the 60s,
the prayer wheels and stupas with
    slanted eyes, the chanting
monks and screaming
    trumpets, the air, the altitude and
giddy humor mixed in with
    theology, demons out of
        caves, mystics
inflamed on ice, huge clouds of
thick green incense, droning
    sound among high crevasses and buttes,
incessant throb of minimal life I
    imagine going up steep and
        narrow stairways to
crag-perched monasteries housing live
mythical beasts with bronze-scaled
        wings, whimsical
monks in brown wool robes giving
quaffs of barley tea out of
        skull teacups to
giant griffins with lightning tails,

or Tahiti, purple isles, bare-breasted
Gauguin natives in languorous ease,
cool lagoons and spumes of volcano smoke,
probably cheapened now by fast-food dumps and
too many French cars,

or Bali, exotic sonorous clatter,
metallic gamelan mystery, green leaves the
size of people flowing from tropical trees,
processions of batik-clad folk with
    platters piled high with petals,
eyes clicking to music, hands angular as
        birds' flight,
dream and reality fused, catching the
    other-worldly screams in
        psychic night,

or Australia, hot and orange, red sky, red
    dirt, people brown with
        red tinge, red hair,
dancing with bowed legs, stamping the
    red dirt, imagery flickering
        across their bodily screens,
more dream-time, natural people
    happily in touch with
        invisible realities,

the many places I may never see,
wilderness of Montana, caves of  Lascaux,
    rock gardens of Kyoto,
Lions of the Serengeti, Kilimanjaro eagles,
    even alligator swamps of

Florida,
and yet there are so many places I have
been and so many things I have seen,
Grand Canyon aged fifteen, Eiffel
    Tower whizzing by in a
Volkswagen bus in a hurry to Morocco,
Morocco and the living saints of
    Algeria, the living saint of
Meknes Morocco who was a mountain
    enough to make earthly mountains
        crumble,
I saw him and did not see him,
his elbow on my knee which felt like a
    tree fallen across it,
an anvil or a planet,

and I've been to Mecca, and sniffed
    original musk of Paradise there,
seen original human beings
    circling its precincts,
heard their one heart beating,

so if I miss anywhere before I die
I've actually been everywhere,
if any physical leaf falls anywhere
my blinking eye perceives it fall.
And if I've missed anywhere
it will enfold me in its globe
as my soul flows into its ennobling and
undifferentiated
        flow.

                                    4/27

## LITTLE BIRD OUT IN THE AIR

There's a little bird
   out in the air
where lightning flashed and
   the thunder that rolled
rolled for a long, long time, some of it
   rumbling still.
Against a backdrop of
   dawn dark sky, this
little bird among the other
   birds I can hear
is calling out with its
distinguishable whistle.
Its name is Dash, and
   like the other birds of its
kind, it is nomadic, lives
in a totally different
   dimension than we
do, sleeps
   where it can,
wakes up to a
   different world each
day, different
tree bough, different
   rooftop, different
city, climate, cuisine.
Maybe it stays near its
   natal neighborhood,
probably not, maybe it
   finds a mate for a
season, then

flies off, maybe it
stays and watches the
    young ones hatch,
bringing them
    delectable bits.
Dash looks out those
    tiny black eyes
and is his own bird.
He flies in the light.
Hunkers down
    in the dark.
Curses no one nor
    anything. Flies
away to a new thing.
    Sings.

5/3

# A STARTLING GREEN LIGHT

## 1

A startling green light glowed in the
  western sky, sizzles of yellow light in
erratic outline preceded it, something
    momentous was coming this way,
something unannounced, irregular,
    out of the ordinary, divine,

starlings flew across our heads in prelude,
babies sat up in their strollers and became
  eloquent,
old men actually sat back in serenity and
  were wise, old
    women likewise,

the tension of time beating our
backs like crazed slave owners
suddenly eased, settled into its
constituents with naturalness, took as
  long as an ant or
  string of ants across a marble
armchair in the park carrying leaves,

a flash of brilliance, a
promise with a freshness in the
  air as if a gospel choir in
    white satin had just
      stood up to a live microphone and
  sung a chord,

everything snapped into deep focus,
foreground objects as
clear as way back, stronger than
starlight, a tone

blew itself into pure existence like a
 noon factory whistle, but this one
was soothing, didn't make black
 cats slink under chairs, but made the
entire natural world relax, fall back
 into itself as if with a smile,

things became anticipatory but not creepy,
suddenly the future was what was coming
 immediately onto the horizon right
in front of us, not in some
 faraway mental gyration, every
leaf-twitch became an
 annunciatory event, every
creak of cedar or oak in the change of
 temperature from one
 degree to the next, every
breath from warm to warmer, or to
 cool from neutral,

the world took on a fictional aspect,
the light on the far horizon widened to a
 sound as of heralding trumpets,

even death became inconsequential-seeming,
 fear of it evaporated, bicycle wheels
 spun on their own,

seeds germinated with a
    universal acceleration,
peoples' concerns were as if
    burned away by hot pokers held
      above them, taking only the
        excessive dross of thwarted
desires and overheated expectations,

what would have normally been a kind of
apocalyptic apprehension, people suddenly
frantic to put their lives in order or do
that thing they'd been sacrificing
    in order to live day to day while
suffering tragically inside, their hearts
    in constant pain and congealment,
instead of this

the anticipation only lengthened the
    breathing-space of the future
      indefinitely, allowed for
everything to take place in its
    own rhythm, things
popped into view and were accepted and
    assimilated without fretfulness or
    ostentation,

the light grew in direct proportion to
    a loving, firm
      voice of clear consciousness invading
every nook and cranny and every
    conscious being in existence,

the light spread across everything in its
path like the rising sun falling across
city buildings and forest trees equally,
equally upon
penniless person awaking in
    anguish among tin cans and
smashed bottles, and
  harmonized son or daughter of deceased
      parents who are as
calm as bees inside their hive
    doing their work,

this light that usually rises in the east and
  sets in the west was
rising in the west now, inching up

moment by moment to fill the
  whole western sky, tingeing
    more and more of the
darkness with a
  supernal radiance like a
    hush filled with portent,

like a room at night
when someone strikes a match...

                                        5/4


**2**


And the faces of our loved ones,
filled as they are with love's radiance,

their eyelids like domes of celestial
architecture floating on lakes,

their eyes, when closed, like the
secrets of saints in the
  deepest chambers of their
    sainthood,

their brows like millenniums so far in the
  future only the
    predictions of the passage of comets
    can be made with any accuracy,

their brows like volumes of early astronomy
bound in leather, printed by
  meticulous hand on vellum, in
      gold ink,

their mouths like the orations of angelic legions
to whole nations of believers,

their lips like the golden roads
Alexander the Great rode out on
with populations of new knowledges
happily heralding him,

they open their eyes like the
  bringing to birth of new
    stallions,
and see the light from the west and are
      unafraid,

they see tents for centuries moved across
   shifting sands, nomadic
      populations telling the
      old stories, singing the
         old songs,

they see the annual migrations of terror and
   mayhem like a rainfall of
      silver spears
      and are unafraid,

they see the earth slowly turning in its
   solar revolutions
      bearing oceanic tides and
         geologic ripplings,
   deep fissures exuding gases, tall
      mountains wreathed in
         cloud,

and see the light arriving with its
hands full of wonders,

its eyes full of worlds of even
greater light coming into
   view...

5/4

**3**

When it finally came
we didn't know what hit us.

We still don't,
but it keeps us alive.

We can't even be sure it has completely arrived.

We can't even be sure what it is
that's arrived.

But a colossal cloud of
energy stood in the air,
and a musical tone,

and tiny tendrils uncurled around it and
rose their full length of
green, and stalks arose
bearing fruit and flower, and
animals cautiously stepped out of
  shadow into light, and
shyness gave way to tentative steps and
slowly became delight, eyes met
  and gestures affirmed
what the heart knew, words were

attempted, preceded by
musical sounds, words of
assurance that what we all
experienced was true, that

what we had anticipated had
  arrived, a
wash of light that rose from the ground
and bathed each thing in glory,

little mouths working in joy of
    ant or butterfly, gnat or the
larger, hairier beasts,

each stepping on earth,
footfalls landing on generous earth,

motions of bodies both in and
    toward the light —

shimmering accelerations of

    pure light!

5/5

## THE PERFECT POEM

What would I sacrifice for the perfect poem?
For my head rising above clouds to
  look along those silver fields of
    vapor, those fluffy diamonds of
light directly at the sun? Would I

throw over my Louis XVI bedside table with its
post-midnight mirror that shows me
    hillsides so green even
      birds won't fly over them,
streams so bright the gliding
  forms of their fish
        reflect in the air?
Would I throw over my steamer trunks of
  carefully folded pelts, bear skins,
    cougar capes, antelope coats with
extra wide sleeves, dolphin jackets and
    antler hats from deep-sea Behemoths
        no one's ever seen?
Should I throw away my Seven Thousand
technicolor ejaculations and my
  two billion ecstatic exhalations?
The delights of my eye
in a fair human form walking on the
sidewalk as I drive by
for a destination forever
    unknown to me, but whose
nonchalance in passing for an instant
      captures my heart?

Should I toss away those
delicious instants in which
snowflakes about to melt on a woolen sleeve
suddenly become giant fountains of
     anti-matter at the exact
          center of the Milky Way, or
sighting along the outermost edge of the
universe, objects that resemble
galloping horses flashing silvery manes
protrude above the flat horizon of space before us?
Do they have to go also?

The imagination's twenty towers of light,
my desire for the prefect utterance, to be
an unstopped flute of
          irrepressible singing that
floats along for days thoroughly open and
     happily unstoppable until the
whole world throws off its clothes and starts
          dancing?
Should that go too?

The ark of this earth is as fragile as balsa.

The ocean of night is fierce and dark.

But the perfect poem, its illuminated head with
     its heart in its hands,
its lips of twin peacocks
opening their tails in the tree of light,
its perfect song a tendril of breath from a
          void that doesn't exist,

its perfect song from the Plenitude of God's
   Generous Mercy on earth
      spread like starlight across a
glass tabletop,

the perfect poem!

Our eyesight flashed to happy blindness

by its sound!

5/7

# A LITTLE RIVER

A little river sang especially hard
in its eagerness to reach the sea,
smashed its waters against rocks
and fell great heights into pools
out of its longing to lose itself
in a body of water inconceivably
    wide and deep
with a sky above it greater than any
   cloudy sky the river sometimes
contemplated as it gurgled along
on a lazy summer day.

A spark of flame cracked and spat in its
   longing to flare up to enormous
bonfire size and
extinguish itself in a burst of
   reddish light, flash hugely enough to
contemplate the dark night around it
then enter that dark night so
   cool and dimensional
    a little spark like itself would
never know its size, but be the
mind of darkness inside greater night
expanded at its
   moment of extinction to the
    very edges of  blackness,
becoming for an inconceivable moment
the entire dimension of night,
from just one spark to
   all darkness itself.

A camel stood next to a pyramid, as
close as possible in ochre Egyptian
        sunlight, proudly lifting its
great camel head in side view next to the
Great Pyramid hoping to get some of its
great pyramid power, closed its
lustrous camel eyes with its
    new moon lashes and
        fell into a reverie centuries
long, shadows of slaves with
tons of stone trudging uphill and
down deep inside him.

A cricket sang in the night.

A frog blew out its
    throat in a membranous ball
and croaked gloriously
in the dark.

A light fell from a high
    window then went out.

A light fell from a height
    then went out.

A light entered the dark
and became the dark.

5/9

## WE SIT IN OUR HOUSES

We sit in our houses, awake, at
  dawn, but
we don't know what's going on.

We don't see the white lions standing at the
city's gates, hummingbirds
hovering by their ears, constellations like
neon signs over their heads,

we don't see the slim politician stuffing his
    pockets full of gold, in the
back of a black limousine driven by
alligators in white tuxedos,
each gold coin minted with the politician's likeness
standing on a pyramid, fake rubies on the ground,

we don't see the ten rivers of milk and honey
rising through our streets, washing through the
    windows of the orphanage, making
recent widows weep,

we don't see the figure of death with rotten
teeth and breath of a blast furnace
    at intersections waiting for green lights
turn to us and sneer,

we don't see what's going on here,
we sit on the sides of our beds with
various prayers, and
God is near, but we don't see

the lone white bird at dawn fly in
    figure eights as the
  sun comes up, and those
figure eights like a choir of light with
tiny flames in the sky opening
    windows in the night,

we don't see in the distance the
bridge of human souls that stretches
    over the abyss, nor the
Behemoth below with fangs of mythology and
the number of our days on
        earth in reality,

we sit in our rooms with outrageously bright tropical
orchids in the Unseen all around us
and butterflies with glistening transparent
    wings and sweet strings of
nectar in the air, gnats with the
faces of our genealogical tree
hovering around a lightbulb,

that we don't see,

we don't see the
door of the future opening and a tall
figure with the face of a cat deliver to us
the sealed letter of our fate, eyes as
    bright as headlights,
who says, "*What you see and
    what you don't see
are both known best by the*

*angel of insight, who*
*stands just inside the Unseen and*
    *listens to your heartbeats like a*
      *good doctor and*
*whispers in your ear*
*to put away all fear."*

We sit in our houses at dawn with the
birds outside becoming clear.

Their hearts are sure.

I hear them at the door.

5/13

# BOARDWALK

There's a funny kind of long horizontal
　　　boardwalk that extends
all down the beach and soaks up the sun
and a single building of fantastic architecture
spans it, with little peaked roofs, domes, turrets,
　　　towers, elongated vertical windows,
crow's-nests as on old sailing ships,

and it sags and creaks,
it's bleached almost white by the sun,
it sits on its wooden foundation and seems to
　　　listen to the lapping waters, some even
sizzling up underneath its massive pilings,
washing up those greenish-brownish brackish
　　　kelp-bulbs that pop when you
　　　　　step on them,

and no one lives in any of the rooms,
well a giant spider lives in one of the rooms, situates
　　　himself smack in the
middle of the floor and has a
human face, cool, almost beatific,
　　　heavy patient eyelids, brow as if
reflective of moonlight,

while a little way down the way is a
room full of garishly painted rubber toys, another full of
gilded Irish harps played on
　　　full moon nights by phantom fingers,
other rooms are ballrooms for the

wearied waltzes of the dead,
other rooms, the largest, harbor
    herds of wild horses, they
charge with faces forward and manes
        fiery, turn as one and gallop
back again, hoofs hammering the
old wooden floorboards as if a new
    earth were being born, or the
        end of the world were in the
process of passing.

I don't know why this image has been
    conjured. It bears no
actual relation to human health or salvation.
I don't see a particular light about to
burst it asunder and explode into the
hearts of readers or listeners.
But there it sits, in some imagined world,
the sea's real, the beach smells of
    bracken and brine, the voices coming
        down from the highway are
real, the children's calls and roundabout
            replies, the
boardwalk itself like a slowly flapping
    banner of itself being
flown over the waves, the
entire beach itself.

For in reality there's only one grain of sand.
And it's just now falling down the
pinched neck of the hourglass.

5/13

# PLEA

## 1

I want to ride a huge blue wave
    to Your Presence, Lord, a
stiff blue wave like a giant meringue
      that blasts through walls,

I want to arrive on one huge foot, Lord
one swift foot that hops up slopes
    to Your most
      intimate precincts,

I want to open a door the
    size of the sky with one smooth
twist of the knob, Lord,
      to let light in,

I want to arrive in silhouette, Lord,
    thin as a vapor,
supple as thread, essential,
      lighter than air,

a face on a stick all eyes for You, Lord,
    silent as space where
blue birds fly to their goals,

I want to arrive on the breath of a tree
      in heavenly regions,
the click of a twig as it falls to the
    ground in a breeze, Lord,

flung to the ground with leaves,
flat as the earth, Lord,
     flashing like glass,
     fast as a flash of light,

first flight of bee to Your
     fragrant flower, Lord,

in first morning light.


**2**


I come to You in the faces of skyscrapers
     twinkling in the sun,

in the thighs of wild horses churning across
          rivers,

in the creak of old mill wheels in rural
     Scandinavia, I come to You, Lord,

unappeased, unanswered,

I come to You in the spinning hubcaps of
     roadsters maneuvering curves,

in the row of newly planted dogwood saplings
     turning tender leaves to the rain,

in puppy faces pinkly scrunched together
in a raffia basket in a circus parked

in a rain-drenched Italian town,

I come to you in the frilly calliope songs of
sparrows and starlings this dawn Philadelphia at
    millennium's end,

I come, Lord, openhanded, openhearted,

I come to You in the snappy trudge of time
that has me white-bearded with straggly
    white chest-hairs and
wrinkled backs of hands
while my 16 year-old daughter and 20 year-old son
    are wide-eyed at life, trying things
        out for the first time, overjoyed,

I come to you in the iceberg's lengthy flash
    of arctic sleep with its profound
        depths and diving penguins,

I come to you in the bicycle spokes of Chinese
    workers crossing the city
        on their way home at dusk, smoking
            American cigarettes,

I come to You, Lord, in as many ways and
    guises as possible for
        fear I might miss You,

in the prairie dogs' yelp as they stand on
    their hind legs and look around,

in the death row's inmate looking up
    from his reading with
        tears in his eyes, astounded,

I come now as raw as the weather on the
    high seas, unready as a

fledgling kicked out of its nest by its
    own mother to make it fly,

I come to you in the gray pebbles at the
    bottom of a stream,

in the overpink cotton candy dwindling in the
    child's hand, by his
        tongue and by the natural evaporation of
            spun sugar in air,

I come to You by the light creeping golden up a canyon's
    rim in Arizona,

by the hurricane underbelly black as
    pitch in the sky above Tulsa,

by the sparkling Moroccan wildflowers as
    bright as if painted by hand,

I come to You, Lord, ashamed and
    unashamed, on my
        knees and standing,
fleshy and fault-ridden, imperfect as

bad pottery thrown by my own hand
with perfect clay provided by You, Lord, beforehand,

unready for the encounter, longing
    for the encounter,

in Your time
and in Your space,

like the natural
curvature of the earth, Lord, half in
    darkness, half in
light, grinding away on my wobbly axis in the
    dark of night,

ready or not, Lord,

I come to You.

5/16

# GONE

The police detectives in their
crisp ironed uniforms will ask
what were my habits, why and when I did
    such-and-such, but
I will be gone.
The forensic expert will measure and sift,
sift and measure, photograph and
    dust like a rare bird
preparing its nest, but
I shall be elsewhere.
The historian (though I flatter myself)
may inquire about my ways and
    wise sayings, when I did
such-and-such, what I
thought about such-and-such,
but I shall be safely out of range.
Neighbors will question each other about the
   time and the day and the
    strange noises, but
me and my strange noises will have
moved on.

A shadow against a rock,
a momentary silencing of crickets,
a splash into a small pond,
the sound of a closing window sash, the
    discreet closing of a screen door,
then the closing of the door itself,
but I will be nowhere in sight,
nowhere in sound or time or space,

just a faint yellow wisp in the air,
just a few thousand notebooks with
    barely decipherable scrawl,
only the utterly perfect inner
    form will remain
        that eluded me all these
years,
actions whose best intentions were
too few, good words like
geese from Canada, stopping to
    beautify a waterway
        then disappear.
Our mortal beings occupied such a
large amount of space and importance
to us, so involved the legions of
    heavenly facilitators, troops of
earthly betrayers and impeders, yet
the house closes easily while the
personal effects are removed,
the furniture is easily discarded, the
struggled-over utterances either
    recorded and perpetuated or
fed to insatiable flames,

but I will be
in as elsewhere an elsewhere as
anywhere else than right here and now is,
inconceivable to us, a land that is
more a dimension, unthinkable, with its
    various treasures,
there I shall be when the
import of these words is realized,

more of an echo than a reality,
though to me finally
 all the reality that
also eluded me while I was alive.
The reality confirmed but by then
  unsayable.
I'll be consigned to Reality with all
  its mercy.
Nonlocateable except within the
  essence of itself.

No forwarding address even remotely possible.

Safely beyond even the
possibility of return.

5/17

# NOW, FOR THE NEXT POEM

OK, for the next poem I'd like to call on
  one thousand and ten blackbirds
  to make configurations in the
sky between your eyes and the sun,
    silhouette messages, writing out
words or showing linear sketches of
    familiar figures in the air. Hydrants.
Umbrellas. The shape of a single huge
    blackbird made out of the
one thousand and ten, outlined and flying
    slowly across to the left.
And underneath, a glass boat. Hull, sides,
    prow, mast, glass, glittering,
    serene, gliding along a glassy sea
and you can look down at aquatic life
    burgeoning underneath,
maybe sunken cities, pillars, seaweed
    big as houses rippling upwards.
So, crows and a scow.
And the sea, of course, the
briny, salty sea, a dark Prussian blue with
flecks of turquoise, silver scallops where
    sunlight hits, and the waves
absolutely still at first, the eerie
sight of the ocean's animation, usually so utterly
    continual, halted, suspended, not like
when Moses in that movie cuts through, water
    furiously pouring upside-down and sideways,
but all the water of the sea frozen in time, then

begun again, rolling and
    roaring.

OK. Now we've got blackbirds, a boat, the
sea set at normal speed, making its usual racket,
and for light I'd like something palatial coming
        right down out of the sky,
stairways with smoking urns, pillars going up
    as infinitely as possible, beyond the
        stretch of human eyesight,
actually disappearing into the clouds,

then bright light bursts out from between
the pillars, golden and lemon yellow,
illuminated blades cutting away all darkness,
and down the steps, a procession of
        personages, I don't know

who, some could be
running, they don't have to be formal and
pompous, in fact I don't even want human forms
        at all, but rather
a menagerie of animals, furry ones,
a bear, slightly goofy, bobbing his pointy snout, sort of
stumbling down the stairs, then

for pomp, a lion, very self-possessed and
self-contained, who might be imagining

all this imagery and activity coming
out of himself, as I do,
from his leonine vantage,

162

when in fact the geometrically sharp perfection of the
stairway is something neither of us

could so exactly conceive, as well as the
thundercloud rolling in from the right that
suddenly bunches together into a
fist of horrific darkness, strikes the
match of a gigantic lightning bolt stretching from
        heaven to earth,

and pours down rain.

5/20

# FLY ON THE WALL

Negotiations for what little was
  left took place in the
shell of the palace, the two parties
    arriving by limousine from opposite
sides of town.

They met in what was left of the
Great Hall, small
  mammals having made it their
residence, and various denizens of the
    insect world, some familiar some
      not, crisscrossed the ceiling and
floor during some of the more
  heated arguments between the
designated negotiators.

When the maps were brought in,
rattling scrolls on metallic parchments
    drawn up by the opposing
      parties,
hordes of lizards whose dwellings were within
the ancient parquet walls scampered out
and stopped mid-scamper to lift and
lower themselves characteristically on their
tiny taloned legs and jaggle their
    prehistoric heads with those
      fierce beady eyes on this
historic occasion.

When the negotiations broke down and the
   furrowed negotiators began frowning
even more than before, keeping teeth-clenched
silences for longer and longer periods,
the ant colony from the West Wing decided to
      transport its
eggs to new ground across the dingy marble
   floors, and they crossed in such
numbers that in the long stone silences of the
      negotiators you could
actually hear legions of tiny feet
         tapping the marble.

Rural towns were up for grabs.
The two sides of the river were in dispute.
The northern provinces and the southern
      provinces certainly couldn't be
         governed by the
same entity! And what about the
official language?

Squinting and
spitting and scanning the ceiling
      began to take the
place of conciliatory words.

Papers began being collected noisily.
Brief cases began snapping shut.
Wing'd insects with long snouts began flying in the
      windows and flurrying around the
negotiator's heads. Inside the
negotiator's heads the bloody heads of their

opponents began appearing on long poles outside the
ruined palace gates, or rolled in a
    violent ball game between ruthless
        teams, kicked into
unrecognizable shapes.

Mandibles gnawed insect parts. Spiders
made intricate corner webs and hammock-like
lace between the legs of
        the ornate chairs.

The great sun itself slid down
into one of these gossamer nets
and left the palace rooms in a fog of
        disarrayed darkness as
the negotiators fell into a silence
        no word could break.

Limousines departed as
cockroaches crossed in the dark.

                    5/21

# THE DAY THE EARTH STOOD STILL

**1**

A hundred cars crashed without sound.
A pin dropped but
    was not heard.
Nothing itched. No one scratched.
No thoughts crossed the mind
the day the earth stood still.

No brick fell.
No leaf fell on pond.
No stone fell against stone.
No girl brushed back tears.
No cat meowed, no dog barked
the day the earth stood still.

No one brought pasha tea.
No bear poked nose into treetrunk.
No bike skidded to a stop.
No ant twitched.
No fluff fell through air
the day the earth stood still.

No window slid down or up.
No birds sang at dawn.
No pen scratched out a poem.
No pebble fell against pebble.
No horse shied.
No owl turned to look
the day the earth stood still.

The day the earth stood still
water didn't run backwards,
words didn't suck back through lips.
Eyes didn't unblink.
Love didn't get unmade.
Nothing got left undone.
No stone left unturned
the day the earth stood still.

5/29

## 2

The baby-faced man folded his napkin just so
the day the earth stood still.

The golden-haired alpinist made a small but
   fatal move
the day the earth stood still.

The Sibyl, crouched behind her rude rock, foretold with
    accuracy and spoke perfect Greek
the day the earth stood still.

The Sicilian locomotive engineer who always wore
   loud ties and spat obscenities
had a lovely thought of his paternal grandmother
as he blew the whistle and rounded a bend
the day the earth stood still.

Two Persian oud players, executing a
long and intricate run in perfect synchronicity,

experienced lift-off at the
    same moment
the day the earth stood still.

The Mayor of the small town of Dukret, Switzerland,
    stepped up to a bank of microphones to
shamelessly lie to the assembled press, and
a ray of sudden sunlight blinded him
the day the earth stood still.

A small, pale-faced chimpanzee peered into
    the room inquisitively just as Edward
      Negomo proposed marriage on bended knee to
Samilele Zuwawee, who glanced up
    just at that moment
the day the earth stood still.

A vulture of prodigious size flew off the
    railroad station roof to the
      collective amazement of the
Croatian townspeople
the day the earth stood still.

God's footprint could be seen as clear as
    day on the surface of the
Mediterranean Sea late afternoon to the
    astounded fishermen
returning home with
    nearly empty nets
the day the earth stood still.

And you came across the empty room
  touching the backs of chairs with your
delicate hands, and your face came up
close to mine and mimed the words
with your lips that were going through
my mind at the same time:
*"The earth is standing still. The*
  *earth is standing exquisitely and*
    *perfectly still!"*

                                        5/30

**3**

This very time and place
assumed its primordial duration and
  spatial perspective with all its
original wild foliage and all the
  stars presently above our heads not
light years old as they are now, but as
young and fresh as they
were at birth

the day the earth stood still.

Matter just as it is (chairs, tables, mugs of tea,
stubby pencils, extended floors, doors that
  open and close) strained at its
confining molecular arrangements until it became
a focus for the vastness of
    celestial influence, all material
    shapes outlined with

silvery rainbows ribbon-thin,
voices singing in all the things around us
  praise-songs to their Creator

the day the earth stood still.

The conundrums of being (basic mortality, breathing
  easily, sexual urges, the urge to
that which we are not or that which we
  have not)
undid themselves like loosely-tied
pinkish noodle-forms, and, as epic as
the Red Sea in its famous unzippering,
paved a way for everyone to see not only
their own liberation from the
  incipient madness of being
but into the loving embrace of
  total effacement
whose core is a light and whose form is a
pure sound that comes before
  world's beginning
    and world's end

the day the earth stood still.

The glittering sky stretched in our
heads and over our heads in the
  limitless air above our
    heads like a million-story
atrium of cloud opened onto
  vistas more spectacular than
    hallucination however benign and more

refreshing than a swim in a secret
Hawaiian grotto at the end of a long trek
    down tropical paths to
nowhere in particular and
      everywhere at once

the day the earth stood still.

The Great Ones whose presence is so
longed for and whose deaths are always an
ark-shaped door in the side of a hill of
    dark rubble
and whose words continue to reverberate with the
poignancy of snowy egrets landing
  briefly on the roofs of farms
just before dusk, white
    feathery wings against night's fields,
the saintly presence of the Great Ones
filled the air with
  photo-realistic etchings of worlds of light
and all the boundaries between
life and death and the living and the
    dead
dissolved

the day the earth stood still.

The day the earth stood still
each living creature's words were deciphered,
each living molecule of existence
  showed the secret crystals of its
patterns on a cosmic scale that easily

fit into the palms of our hands,
I was there and you were there
and nothing was left to be revealed
for the earth stood still as it
    always does,

for they talk of cosmic chaos and
galactic turmoil, but from my
garden in Philadelphia as the sun goes down

(as the lumbering globe turns away from the
sun to plunge us in darkness)

the black cat in the house scratches at the screen door
    to come out, birds are calling
polyphonically to each other before darkness
    envelopes them,

grass and leaves of plants and weeds
flitter a little in the evening breeze,

and the earth stands still,

car-tires boom down the street at the
end of the alley, or pass as
one did just now with pneumatic wheeze,

and the earth stands still,

its windows filled with pictures,
pictures pass, but the

earth stands still

beholding its movement with
perfect poise and balance.

*Swing birds,*
*    that perfect music!*

*All across the*
*evening space of earth's stillness.*

*Sing as I do*
*as the sun goes down*

*and the earth stands still!*

5/30